Giants for Justice

Other books by the same author

🏀

Martin Luther King, Jr.
Muhammad Ali
The Great Minu
Stevie Wonder

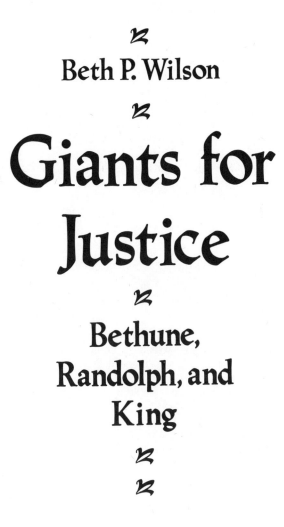

Beth P. Wilson

Giants for Justice

Bethune,
Randolph, and
King

New York and London
Harcourt Brace Jovanovich

Printed in the United States of America

Library of Congress Cataloging in Publication Data

Wilson, Beth P
Giants for justice: Bethune, Randolph, and King.

Includes bibliographies and index.
SUMMARY: Biographical sketches of three outstanding black leaders who did much
to pave the way toward dignity and freedom for their people in education, labor,
and civil rights.

1. Afro-Americans—Biography—Juvenile literature. 2. Bethune, Mary
Jane McLeod, 1875–1955—Juvenile literature. 3. Randolph, Asa Philip,
1889– —Juvenile literature. 4. King, Martin Luther—Juvenile literature.
[1. Bethune, Mary McLeod, 1875–1955. 2. Randolph, Asa Philip, 1889– 3.
King, Martin Luther. 4. Afro-Americans—Biography] I. Title.
E185.96.W65   920'.073 [920]   77-88971
ISBN 0-15-230781-8

First edition

B C D E F G H I J K

Remembering my mother and father
who spent long years
in the cause of justice

Contents

Ʀ

Martin Luther King, Jr.

ACKNOWLEDGMENTS

Special thanks to Mr. A. Philip Randolph for his assistance, to Mr. C. L. Dellums, who read the Randolph section of the manuscript, to Mrs. Mabel Jackson, Committee of "400," National Council of Negro Women, and to my husband, Dr. W. D. Wilson, whose support helped make this book possible.

Introduction

ϰ

In the struggle of any people to free themselves from oppression, there always emerge a few courageous ones who lead.

Before and after the Civil War in the United States, fearless Blacks, such as Harriet Tubman, Sojourner Truth, Frederick Douglass, and Booker T. Washington, gave strength and courage to Black Americans on their tortuous road toward freedom.

In the twentieth century, there were three remarkable leaders whose work spanned a period of about seventy-five years. Mary McLeod Bethune, A. Philip Randolph, and Martin Luther King, Jr. knew and supported each other, but more important, they all embraced a commitment to help meet the three greatest needs of American Blacks in this century—better education, better and more secure jobs, and better laws to protect their human rights.

I have chosen to include these "giants for justice" in one book because I was struck not only by the fact that their missions were uniquely interrelated, but by the power and impact of their cumulative efforts.

Mary McLeod Bethune

𝕫

" 'If you burn my buildings, I'll build
them again. And if you burn them a
second time, I'll build them back again!'
The startled Klansmen sat on their
horses motionless. Then they turned
and rode off."

𝕫

Growing Up in Mayesville

🗲

NIGHT CAME to a cotton plantation near the little town of Mayesville, South Carolina, in 1885. Ten-year-old Mary Jane McLeod moved about the sitting room of a four-room wooden cabin. She lit a kerosene lamp. Then she opened the Holy Bible that the Reverend Bowen had given the family. Mary Jane wondered what all those words meant, and she prayed to God that she would learn to read one day.

Later in the evening, the family would gather, led by Grandmother Sophia, who put down her corncob pipe and sat humming in her rocking chair. Then came Mary Jane's parents, Patsy and Samuel McLeod, with the younger children. The older ones had grown up and gone away. Mr. McLeod stood holding the Bible open, even though he couldn't read. Then, after singing "Swing Low, Sweet Chariot," the family would kneel in prayer.

Grandmother Sophia, Patsy and Sam McLeod had been slaves until the Emancipation Proclamation in 1863. And slaves had not been taught to read because their masters, except for a very few, felt that they might cause trouble or run away if they had any education. Mary Jane, born July 19, 1875, was a "free" child, but there was no school for Black people in Mayesville, and no one to teach her.

The McLeods were a loving family. Sam McLeod, Mary Jane's father, had fallen in love with a tall and stately slave woman called Patsy, who worked on a nearby plantation. He told Mr. McLeod, his master, that he wanted to marry her, and McLeod permitted Sam, a good-natured and dependable man, to work extra hours both for him and for other planters so that he could buy his bride.

The first fourteen of their seventeen children were born on the McLeod plantation. But even after the Emancipation Proclamation, Patsy and Sam remained on the McLeod land as sharecroppers. They were given food and shelter and, after the harvest, a share of the crops in return for their work. Patsy continued to work for her former owner, Ben Wilson, until she earned enough money to purchase five acres of land from him. Later, Sam and Patsy were able to buy thirty more acres by working long hours the year round. Sam and his oldest sons then proudly built the log cabin in which Mary Jane, his fifteenth child, was born.

Under the sharecropping system, landowners would often cheat the sharecropper who couldn't figure quantities in any given crop. This kept the farmer in debt to the planter year after year. If he tried to seek justice, he would lose his court case because a Negro's testimony was not accepted. In a way, this was worse than slavery because the farmer was supposed to be a free man.

The McLeods worked from early morning to dusk, happy to have such a large farm and to be free and independent. Everyone worked on the farm except Grandmother Sophia, who knitted and helped in other ways. They planted vegetables and rice. And they grew cotton—some for clothing, but mostly to sell. The only time during the day that they took a break was when Patsy McLeod called them in for a hearty lunch, usually of black-eyed peas and cornbread.

In the evening, Mary would often snuggle against her grandmother before the open fire, ready for a story. Grandmother Sophia would tell about their royal African ancestors who lived in Guinea in West Central Africa.

Chiefs ruled the tribal families in the villages. These families raised cattle on pastures that spread out for miles. On ceremonial days, these proud people wore fine clothing and gold or ivory bracelets. Mary Jane's eyes sparkled when she was told how the families gathered around to tell stories and to dance. Sometimes they did tribal dances all night long. But all that had happened before slave traders stole Grandmother Sophia's mother away from Africa and sold her on the slave block in America.

Everyone said that Mary Jane must have been born with her eyes wide open because she was so alert. When she was quite small, she had learned to ride Old Bush, the family mule, and had helped with the plowing. By the time she was seven, she was inspired by her mother—who kept small tin cans with slits in them to encourage her children to save the pennies they earned selling plums or berries—to organize the local Black and white children into a Tin Can Banking Circle. She told them to save their pennies in cans so they could give Christmas gifts to other children. This, she said in her small, forceful voice, would be much more fun than spending all the money on candy for themselves. When the cans were opened before Christmas, the children were surprised to see how much they had saved.

The hard winter months stretched on, but the McLeods kept working. Soon it was plowing time again. When the new cotton season started, the battle with crab grass began. The family was constantly hoeing to keep the crab grass away from the young, tender plants. Mary Jane always sang as she worked. Sometimes she would stop to pray right in the field. "Please God," she would say, "help me get away from this crab grass. Help me learn to read."

In October 1886, Mary Jane trudged down a dirt road to the general store carrying a heavy sack of hickory nuts to be exchanged for sugar and lard. The Black preacher had left a message at the store for Mrs. McLeod. The storekeeper said it was about some mission school that was going to open in Mayesville. Mary was so excited she ran flying home with the news.

The family talked the matter over. They knew how Mary longed to read. They knew how bright she was and felt that she should have the chance to go to school. But they needed her so badly on the farm. She could pick 250 pounds of cotton in a day! The room grew still as they tried to reach a decision. Then Grandmother Sophia, puffing on her pipe, said in a firm voice, "Send that child to school! She's goin' to amount to somethin' someday, praise God." As her parents nodded in agreement, Mary Jane jumped up and down for joy.

Mary Jane had to walk five miles down a dusty road to the old wooden schoolhouse, but the long walk didn't discourage her because she was too happy to feel tired. She loved school. And she loved the Black teacher, Miss Wilson. She became a good reader and moved faster than the boys in arithmetic. Although the school was only open a few months of the year, Mary Jane was able to help Miss Wilson with the new pupils in no time at all.

Mary Jane read the Bible to the family and to anyone else who came to listen. She taught her brothers and sisters to read. And she helped her father and neighbors, both Black and white, with their arithmetic. They had to know the weight and price of cotton and their share of the crop so they wouldn't be cheated. They also had to know how to figure the amount of their bills at the village store.

Even after most sharecroppers had finally paid off their debts, grocers or other merchants would often shortchange them. One day, when Mary Jane went to the store with her father, she politely asked the grocer to add the figures again. This kept Mr. McLeod from being overcharged for his supplies.

By the end of her second year, Mary Jane was ready to receive her certificate from the mission school. Like the other girls, she wore her first frilly white dress with a blue sash, but her imposing appearance and eagerness made her stand out from the rest.

Oh, To Be a Missionary!

𝜡

In 1887, Miss Mary Crissman, a Quaker dressmaker from Denver, Colorado, offered her savings to the mission school so that a promising Black child could get an education. When news of the scholarship reached the school, Miss Wilson selected Mary Jane, and together they rushed to the McLeod cabin, where everyone rejoiced.

Weeks earlier, Mary Jane had heard a visiting preacher speak at the Methodist church in Mayesville. He had said that missionaries must be sent to spread the gospel of Jesus Christ among the neglected Africans. Then and there she decided that one day she would go to Africa as a missionary.

In September, Mary Jane, the little country girl with braids, left for Scotia Seminary, a Presbyterian church school in Concord, North Carolina. Everyone was so excited for her. Nearly half of Mayesville appeared to wave good-bye at the railroad station.

At the seminary, Mary Jane ate with a fork for the first time. And when she was shown her bedroom, she cried, "Is this big room just for me and another girl?" She looked with amazement as she walked around the three-story brick building and the chapel next door, named Faith Hall. There were Black and white teachers at Scotia, and everyone seemed friendly. Two white teachers helped Mary Jane to adjust to her new world and talked over matters that troubled her.

Mary Jane studied hard. She learned the history of Black people in America as well as world history. She became a forceful and convincing speaker on the debating team. And everyone loved her sense of humor! To help pay her way, she worked in the school laundry and helped in the kitchen.

Seven happy years passed quickly, and Mary's many friends were sorry when the time came for her to leave.

Because Mary Jane graduated with such a good record, Miss Crissman announced that she would be given still another scholarship! She had dreamed of becoming a missionary in Africa for so long. Now she would be able to attend Bible school and prepare for her life's work.

Mary Jane's family and all the well-wishers who had waved good-bye to a little country girl welcomed home a poised young lady eager to share her education. She gave lessons in reading and arithmetic three times a week for anyone who was interested. And, with her rich voice, she conducted group singing, which everyone loved. The McLeods had never been so proud.

Later in September, Mary Jane entered Moody Bible Institute in Chicago, Illinois. Chinese, Japanese, and Indian missionaries were enrolled at the institute, but the only Black students at that time were Mary and one young African. Dwight L. Moody, a tall, heavy-set man, who founded the school, taught his students to love and serve all people, Black or white, rich or poor.

Mary Jane took her studies seriously at Moody. She especially enjoyed the musical training because she loved to sing. She liked doing field work, too—visiting and helping the people in the poorer sections of Chicago. She sang and read the Bible to the old and offered comfort to those in sorrow. She was nearly twenty years old by this time and could picture herself doing the work she loved in Africa. When her missionary course was nearly completed, she applied for an assignment.

Then a letter came from home bringing bad news.

Mary Jane stood frozen as she read it. The McLeod cabin, built of dry pine, had caught fire and burned to the ground. The family, already deep in debt, would need to borrow more money to build a new one. How would she find a way to help? Soon the words came to her: "Pray for another miracle."

A few days later, she was asked to report to the school office. This would be her missionary appointment! She rushed down the hall and into the office. There she found a group of women, but they were not from a mission board. They told her they had heard her beautiful voice and asked her to sing at a large affair. Mary Jane hid her disappointment and graciously consented.

The miracle came soon after, when Mary Jane received a letter and a check for forty dollars for her performance. She didn't stop to wonder what to do with the check. She sent it at once to her parents to help pay for building the new cabin.

After graduation, Mary Jane went to New York to ask the Presbyterian Board of Missions for an assignment in Africa. Other graduates had already been given travel money and were leaving for foreign service. But not Mary Jane McLeod. The Board of Missions told her gently that there was no opening for a Black missionary in Africa at that time.

She walked away, trying to hold back choking sobs. She spoke softly to herself. "I'm not going to be assigned? Not going to Africa to serve the people Grandmother Sophia told me were my own?"

After suffering through her great disappointment, Mary's thoughts began to take a new turn. After all, her people lived in America, too. And there was no doubt that she could serve them as well—perhaps even better. She thought about the unfair laws in the South, about poor schools, poor jobs, and the lack of doctors for Black people in Mayesville. She thought about the Ku Klux Klan, whose members rode at night, covered with white sheets like ghosts, to frighten and terrorize innocent Blacks. Sometimes they would snatch a person off the road at random and viciously beat him. It became clearer than ever to her that her people needed her *here,* in America.

In September 1895, Mary Jane accepted a teaching position at Haines Normal Institute in Augusta, Georgia. She became an excellent teacher, working with her students as their friend as well as their mentor. And when she joined the school choir, both teachers and students enjoyed her lovely voice and warm personality.

Mary Jane had boundless energy and needed little sleep. On weekends, she visited her students' families and taught younger children in the neighborhood. She also kept in close touch with her own family, sending most of her salary home so that her two younger sisters could attend Scotia Seminary, as she had done.

One evening Mary Jane met a tall, handsome young man at choir rehearsal. His name was Albertus Bethune, and he was also a teacher. They both enjoyed singing and reading poetry. They began to see a great deal of each other. Albertus even taught Mary to ride a bicycle! Soon they fell in love and were married.

Mary Bethune worked by day and dreamed at night. She worried about the millions of American Black people who had no education. One evening she said to Albertus, "There are so *many* to teach. Why not start a school of our own?" But Albertus only wanted to teach, not run a school. Later on, after their son, Albert, was born, Albertus was surer than ever that his wife was foolish to want the responsibility of a school.

Over the next five years, Mary tried harder than ever to interest Albertus in her plan. Finally, convinced that she never would, she bundled up little Albert and set out for Daytona Beach, Florida. She would start her own school! She had pleaded with her husband to join them soon. Now it was up to him.

A School of Her Own

ʑ

MARY MCLEOD BETHUNE arrived in Daytona Beach with one dollar and fifty cents. That, with faith in God and in herself, was all that she possessed. She walked around town until she came to a run-down, two-story cottage by the city dump. "Maybe I could start there," she thought. She told the owner of the cottage about her plans for a school. She asked him to trust her until she could raise some money, and he agreed.

Mrs. Bethune went from door to door asking for discarded lamps and old dishes. She found a cracked mirror at the dump. Then she asked Black carpenters and painters to help her get the cottage ready. They set up wooden boxes for tables and chairs, and wrapping paper to write on and charred wooden sticks for pencils. Mrs. Bethune baked pies and sold them to Black men who worked on the railroad tracks. Then she began to ask the white people across town for money.

On October 3, 1904, Daytona Educational and Industrial Training School for Negro Girls opened, with Mary McLeod Bethune as principal! Five little girls, whose parents paid fifty cents a week for their schooling, were enrolled. There was one boy—Albert Bethune, Jr.

Classes began in the morning with Bible study, followed by reading, spelling, arithmetic, and sewing. In the afternoon, Mrs. Bethune and the children made and sold sweet-potato pies to earn money for the school's upkeep.

As the months passed, Mrs. Bethune realized that there simply was not enough money to keep the school open. Even though she faced insults many times as a Black woman in the South, she still determinedly rode her bicycle around town once a week asking for donations. When a large hotel opened, she marched her pupils over to sing for its wealthy guests.

But Mary Bethune knew she would have to make substantial contacts in order to move ahead. She knew that rich tourists came South for the winter, but how could she approach them—and who were they? Before long, Black hotel maids and gardeners were giving her the names of many friendly visitors. Soon she was able to make an appointment to see a Mr. James Gamble of Proctor & Gamble Soap Manufacturing Company. Mr. Gamble thought a white person had made the appointment, but decided to listen anyway when they met.

Mary Bethune's eyes flashed with enthusiasm when she told him about her school. When Mr. Gamble showed interest, she invited him to come and visit. The next day, this tall, white-haired man was shocked when he saw the cottage. He turned to this young woman, with her full brown face and thick black hair, and asked, "But where is your school?"

Suddenly she realized that she had described the school she *hoped* to build. "In my mind, in my heart," she said humbly.

Mr. Gamble was so impressed that he gave her a check for $150. And he promised to become a trustee and help to manage the school.

Soon a powerful group was organized by Mr. Gamble to help with the school's development. It consisted of him as chairman, the mayor, two Black ministers, and a realtor. Black mothers came to the school to help with the cooking and cleaning. Black men did carpentry and repair work, and a club whose members were wealthy white women assisted in many ways.

Mary Bethune and her singing group later met Mr. John D. Rockefeller at one of the hotels. Mr. Rockefeller always requested spirituals, and after the group sang he would give each child a shiny dime. Later, he and his son John D., Jr., became staunch friends of Mrs. Bethune's and donated large sums of money to her school.

When Faith Hall, the first building, was erected, Mrs. Bethune's dream was becoming a reality. The air was filled with excitement as students hurried about setting things in order. Across from Faith Hall was the school's vegetable and flower garden, planted and cared for by the students. Mrs. Flora Curtis, an easterner, came South once a year. She visited the school garden every few days and carefully selected ten cents' worth of carrots. But she never had much to say. Then, after an absence of several years, she appeared once and asked to see Mrs. Bethune in her office. She wanted to see her account of purchases over the years. Mrs. Bethune could account for every penny, and Mrs. Curtis seemed to be satisfied. When she died, she left the school more than $40,000. Mrs. Bethune, who had learned to save and spend pennies wisely as a small child, continued to manage money well throughout her life.

One day, after sorting through her bills, Mrs. Bethune and her pupils went to sing at the Palmetto Hotel. They were disappointed to see only a small audience in the lobby. After the program, Mrs. Bethune passed out cards with the address of the school. Then they passed the basket for contributions. A man with blue eyes and a distinguished beard dropped in a twenty-dollar bill!

Weeks later, while Mrs. Bethune was peddling her bicycle down the road, a large car pulled up beside her. Inside was Mr. Thomas H. White of Cleveland, Ohio, manufacturer of White Sewing Machines. He introduced himself and said he remembered her fine singing group at the Palmetto Hotel. It was he who had given the twenty dollars. He later visited her school. During his visit, he noticed a Singer sewing machine that needed repair. So he decided to send Mrs. Bethune several new White sewing machines and gave her $200 as well. He also sent food, warm blankets, and more money, and told her to call upon him if she ever got into a tight spot. Although she never did call upon him, Mr. White continued to give large sums for the purchase of more land and buildings. Once, he and Mr. Gamble donated the entire amount needed for a new building. When Mr. White died, he left the school a trust fund of $67,000.

Now Mrs. Bethune was struggling to provide 250 girls with needed food and clothing as well as an education. She taught them good manners and insisted on cleanliness, promptness, and good study habits. The girls loved her and called her "Mother Bethune." After evening prayers, they would often gather together and talk about Black and white people, and ask her questions about the unfair laws in the South—questions she found difficult to answer.

Meanwhile, her husband had made several extended visits to see her and their son. He praised his wife for her splendid work, helped at the school, and sang in the choir. At one time he left his teaching post to join his family because he missed them so much. He found a job driving a horse and buggy. But eventually he decided to return to teaching, where he could earn more money—part of which he sent to Mary for the school. Still, with every letter, Albertus could feel the gap widening between him and Mary. Her school meant everything to her. Finally, after ten years of marriage, the Bethunes separated permanently. Albert stayed with his mother during his growing-up years. She sent him to Haines Institute for his high school education, then on to Morehouse College in Atlanta, Georgia.

Mrs. Bethune continued to travel around the state, making speeches to raise funds, gaining new friends along the way. Sometimes she took a singing group along because she knew that white people enjoyed hearing spirituals. In her absence, Mrs. Frances Keyser and other trusted teachers operated the school, and Frank Taylor directed work on the school farm, and looked after all of them.

Eventually, a few boys were admitted to the school. With more pupils to care for, the struggle to keep the school open became more difficult. More salaries had to be paid, and there were constant repairs that had to be made. There seemed to be nothing but bills! Then two special visitors gave Mrs. Bethune the courage to go on trying.

The first was Booker T. Washington, who stopped by during a speaking tour. The year was 1908. He had started his own school, Tuskegee Institute in Alabama, with one teacher and thirty students. Now the school had thousands of graduates and sixty buildings. After looking around, he shook his head and told Mrs. Bethune, "It won't be easy. But you will do it."

The second visitor was her mother, slender and white-haired. Mr. McLeod had died, and Mrs. McLeod longed to see her daughter and her grandson. Mrs. Bethune had sent the fare for her mother's first train ride.

The two women embraced with tears of happiness. After walking around the grounds of the school, they went to the auditorium for graduation exercises. Mrs. Bethune told the graduates, "You boys and girls can dream of doing anything! Then, with faith and hard work, you can make those dreams come true." As Mrs. McLeod watched her daughter passing out one diploma after another, she remembered Grandmother Sophia's words when Mary was a child: "She's going to amount to somethin' someday, praise God."

Mrs. Bethune not only went to the community to seek help for her school, but she worked in the community as well. She gave spiritual guidance and held classes for Black men and women in managing their homes and families. Once she held a baby conference so that mothers could show how well they were caring for their babies. Another time, she held a farm contest and gave a prize of a hoe and rake to the family with the best-kept house and farm. And the Sunday afternoon community meetings, started after Faith Hall was completed, were still drawing large crowds of Black and white people. The whites were drawn by the choir singing, but they were timid at first because of the segregation laws. But Mrs. Bethune welcomed them and said, "Sit anywhere. There are no special seats."

A Hospital
for All People

z

MARY BETHUNE'S anger brought about change more than once. One day she saw a little girl doubled over in pain, probably from appendicitis. Mrs. Bethune decided that she had to be rushed to a hospital. But there were no hospitals nearby for Black people. She looked down at the suffering child, and minutes later she stood before a Dr. Bahannon, head of a private white hospital only a few blocks away. She pleaded with him to operate and save the little girl's life.

Dr. Bahannon explained that he couldn't admit the child to the operating room because she was Black. But when he could stand Mrs. Bethune's searching gaze no longer, he took the child to an upper porch and performed the operation there. Later he admitted that he didn't approve of the foolish laws in the South and promised to help Mrs. Bethune and her students in any emergency.

Mrs. Bethune expressed her gratitude. Then she said, "There should be a hospital for all people. With God's help I will erect one myself!" She talked to groups of white people about the unfair laws. And she sent letters all over the country explaining her project and asking for help.

One disappointment followed another, but Mary McLeod Bethune would not give up. A few years later, with the help of young Dr. T. A. Adams, the only Black doctor in town, a small, well-equipped hospital opened its doors—to all races. Many people had contributed money to the building fund, including Thomas White and James Gamble, two of the largest benefactors. Mrs. Bethune named it McLeod Hospital in memory of her father. Both Black and white doctors treated patients in the twenty-bed building, and "Mother Bethune's" own student nurses cared for the sick and the injured. As he had promised, Dr. Bahannon was one of the white doctors who gave assistance when the hospital opened.

News began to spread about this dynamic woman, and soon Mrs. Bethune was accepting speaking engagements around the country. She never failed to thrill her audiences and give her people new hope. These tours also brought hundreds of contributions to the school.

As more Black pupils became educated, more threats came from members of the Ku Klux Klan, who were trying to keep the students from standing up for their rights. Sometimes the Blacks were beaten and killed, and their homes, schools, and churches were burned.

An election was about to be held in Daytona. Bills were to be voted on that would benefit the Black community— one would give them a high school, and another would provide better streets and lighting in the Black district. The Klansmen wanted to defeat the bills, elect their own leaders, and run the city government as they pleased, so they tried to keep the Black people from voting.

The Klan especially hated Mrs. Bethune because she urged Black people to vote. Speaking at a large meeting, she told her people, "Don't be afraid of the Klan! Hold your heads up high. Go without food if you must, but vote!" Then, dressed in white, she returned to her school and crossed the grounds with a determined step. Everyone knew that something was about to happen!

The night before the election, the Klan circled the school with their blazing torches, their angry howls mak-

ing ugly sounds. But they couldn't turn this brave woman
around. She called to her frightened teachers and students. "Turn on all the lights and sing!" As the singing
began, she asked God to protect her. Then she stepped
out on the front porch and faced the mob. She pointed a
trembling finger and said, "If you burn my buildings, I'll
build them again. And if you burn them a second time,
I'll build them back again!"

The startled Klansmen sat motionless on their horses.
Then they turned and rode off. The next day, one
hundred Black citizens of Daytona Beach, Florida,
marched to the polls, led by Mary McLeod Bethune. And
they won the election! Papers across the nation carried
news of their victory and of this fearless woman.

When asked what more the Black person wanted, Mrs.
Bethune replied, "Protection that is guaranteed by the
Constitution of the United States and which he has a
right to expect; the opportunity for development equal to
that of any other American; to be understood; and finally, to make an appreciable contribution to the growth
of a better America and a better world."

In 1925, the school united with a boys' school and became Bethune-Cookman College. New courses were offered, and students were given two years of training after
high school.

Now, for the first time, money worries were not so
great, and Mrs. Bethune, who had worked long hours for
so many years, realized she needed a rest. Friends celebrated her fiftieth birthday with a gift of money so she
could visit Europe. There she was welcomed by statesmen
and royalty, and she received well-deserved honors from
countries all over the world!

To Serve and to Serve

𝕫

In 1928, hundreds of women met in California, where the National Association of Colored Women was holding a convention. They elected Mary McLeod Bethune president. Mrs. Bethune told the women of her great love for young people and said it was the women of America who must guide them. On the platform sat an elderly white lady who listened to the speaker and smiled. When Mrs. Bethune finished her speech, she received a large bouquet of flowers. She accepted it with thanks and then, as the applause rang out, she turned and placed the flowers into the arms of this slender smiling lady. It was Miss Mary Crissman, the dressmaker who had given her the scholarships to Scotia Seminary and to Moody Bible Institute.

Mrs. Bethune worked not only to help Black people; she worked for harmony among the races as well. She became a board member of the National Urban League, an interracial organization that worked to improve living and working conditions for Black people. She also became vice-president of the National Association for the Advancement of Colored People (NAACP), whose Black and white members worked together to protect everyone's human and civil rights. This organization awarded Mrs. Bethune the coveted Spingarn Medal, presented to an outstanding person each year for exceptional service to mankind.

Meanwhile, President Franklin D. Roosevelt had learned about Mrs. Bethune's work, and during the 1930's depression, when millions of Americans had little money and no work, he called her to the White House in Washington, D.C., to ask her to serve as director of Minority Affairs of the National Youth Administration. But she couldn't accept this position and remain president of Bethune-Cookman College, too. She loved her school and didn't want to leave it. But she said, "If my country needs me, I will serve." When the new college head was named, "Mother Bethune" became honorary president.

Mrs. Bethune made it possible for thousands of young people to return to school or to get jobs. She discussed their problems as a friend and returned to visit them from time to time. Her task was difficult, and she had many conferences with President Roosevelt to deal with these problems. As time passed, she and the Roosevelts became good friends. Once the President told her, "You are one person I am glad to see. You never ask anything for yourself but always for others."

Mary McLeod Bethune was busier now than she had ever been in her life. Still she had another idea! It was to organize Black women's clubs and church and business groups into one large body. United, the women of America could accomplish more and make the country a better place for everyone. She talked to many groups as she traveled around the country, and the idea caught on quickly.

In 1935, thirty-five women met in New York City and formed the National Council of Negro Women. The cheering members elected Mrs. Bethune president. After the first year, the council grew rapidly. By 1941, the members felt they had to have a national office. Mrs. Bethune realized that the more members an organization had and the more money they could raise, the easier it would be to attract even more members and more money for greater accomplishments.

Mrs. Bethune thought of Mr. Marshall Field III, founder of the famous Chicago department store, who had worked with her at one time to help improve race relations. She went to Chicago to talk with him, explaining how badly the council needed money for a clubhouse. The members had raised $800 so far, and she asked if he would be willing to make a contribution.

Mr. Field didn't know anything about the council, but he respected Mrs. Bethune and the things she stood for. He immediately wrote a check for $10,000. As Mrs. Bethune thanked him, she thought how proud she was to know white Americans like writer Harrison Rhodes, banker-philanthropist George F. Peabody, and others, who were sincere in trying to correct the wrongs of the past. In 1943, the National Council of Negro Women moved into their clubhouse in Washington, D.C., which they called the Council House.

At about this time, Mrs. Bethune became president of the Association for the Study of Negro Life and History. She assisted the Black historian Carter G. Woodson in collecting and organizing material about Black people, for knowing about the contributions of their forefathers would help Black Americans understand their true worth and would encourage white people to have more respect for their Black brothers.

In 1942, during World War II, Mrs. Bethune became assistant director of the Women's Army Training Corps. She helped to select and advise young women who wanted to serve their country. She made sure that white and Black women received the same training and treatment. Thousands of young people depended upon her guidance and considered her a friend. Many of them continued to send her letters long after the war was over.

In 1945, Mrs. Bethune was nearly seventy years of age. Her health was good, but she had been advised to slow down and to guard against eating sweets. (This was not easy for her. Sometimes she would take a piece of candy, hidden in her pocket, and slip it into her mouth!) She longed to return to her cottage on Bethune-Cookman campus. But she still had important work to do.

That year, fifty nations sent representatives to San Francisco to form a world organization for peace, called the United Nations. People everywhere had become weary of wars and bloodshed. Mrs. Bethune was asked to serve as an official consultant by the State Department, and she brought much experience and understanding to their discussions. She asked the delegates not to forget the man at the bottom of the ladder, no matter what his color or religion might be, since all people are needed to make a peaceful world.

While men and women planned for peace, news came of President Roosevelt's death. People cried openly, and a sadness settled over the country. Mrs. Bethune was among the millions who had lost a friend. Only then did she ask for something for herself—President Roosevelt's silver-headed cane, which Mrs. Roosevelt was happy to give her. (For years Mrs. Bethune had enjoyed the hobby of collecting model elephants, photographs of outstanding men and women, and walking canes of famous men. Now, because of her friendship with President Roosevelt, his cane became particularly special. She used it the rest of her life.)

By 1947, Bethune-Cookman had become a four-year college with an "A" rating from the State Department of Education. Nearly a thousand students were enrolled, including those in the evening school. Hundreds of graduates continued to leave each year, "to serve."

Mrs. Bethune had received eleven honorary degrees from United States colleges. One degree came from Rollins, a white college in Florida. These degrees honored her many years of service to Black youth and to her country. However, the title "Doctor" held no special interest for her. She still preferred and loved the ring of her three names together—Mary McLeod Bethune.

Cabin in which Mary McLeod Bethune was born, July 10, 1875, in
Mayesville, South Carolina

Mary Bethune with a group of students where she first taught school
in Palatka, Florida, c. 1900

Early school farm scene in Daytona Beach, Florida, in 1911. Students are grinding

Mary Bethune with
Eleanor Roosevelt on
her first visit to
Bethune-Cookman
College, April, 1942

sugar cane, and Mary Bethune is shown in the background on the left holding a pail.

Mary Bethune's seventy-fifth birthday celebration at Bethune-Cookman College, Daytona Beach, Florida, July 10, 1950; *(left to right)* son Albert M. Bethune, Sr., grandson Albert M. Bethune, Jr., Mrs. Bethune, niece Georgia McLeod, and foster son Edward Rodriguez

◀

Mary Bethune receiving an honorary Doctor of Humanities degree at Rollins College, Winter Park, Florida, in 1949, the first black woman to be so honored

Mary McLeod Bethune monument, Lincoln Park, Washington, D.C.

Bethune-Cookman College

Memorial
to a Great Woman

ϡ

Mrs. Bethune's doctors were now pleading with her to take an extended rest. In 1949, she took a short trip to Haiti, where she was a guest of the government and received its highest award, the Gold Medal of Honor and Merit. On her return home, she stepped aside to allow Dr. Dorothy Boulding Ferebee to become the new president of the National Council of Negro Women.

Finally, Mrs. Bethune returned to Daytona in 1950. She traveled little but continued to offer counsel as the program of the National Council of Negro Women expanded. Letters came to her from everywhere, and she answered them faithfully.

In 1953, she visited Liberia as the United States representative to the inauguration of President Tubman. This was the first time she had set foot on African soil, and she felt great pride in being an American of African ancestry.

The Supreme Court of the United States made an important decision in 1954. It declared that it was wrong to force Black and white children to attend separate schools. This ruling would give American families a better chance to live as neighbors and friends. When the news reached Mrs. Bethune, she rejoiced and said, "I still have faith in God and in my country that everything will work out right."

Mary McLeod Bethune died the following year. She had worked all her life for a better America and for a peaceful world. She loved all people—young and old, rich and poor, white and Black, all of whom felt a great loss when she died. But they will always remember the stirring words of her will:

> "I leave you love, I leave
> you hope,—I leave you a
> thirst for education,—I
> leave you faith, I leave you
> racial dignity, I leave you
> a desire to live harmoniously
> with your fellow man, I leave
> you, finally, a responsibility
> to our young people."

So simple a life to cast a lasting afterglow.

Afterword

ↄ

In 1957, Dorothy I. Height became president of the National Council of Negro Women. With great hope and faith, she began to lead the council in a dignified and capable manner.

Several years later, women of all races and religions began to raise money for a monument to the memory of Mrs. Bethune. Author-journalist Ida M. Tarbell had listed her as one of fifty great living American women. Both small and large sums were collected so everyone could share in the project. This undertaking required much planning and money. Several times it became necessary to secure a time extension from Congress, since the monument was to be erected on public land.

Finally, in 1971, ground-breaking ceremonies took place at the east end of Lincoln Park in Washington, D.C. This marked the beginning of the first memorial to a Black American in a public park in the nation's capital.

On July 10, 1974, the dedication and unveiling took place. The beautiful bronze statue shows Mary McLeod Bethune looking into the future as she passes her legacy of love to a girl and a boy. The figures, standing on a 20-foot wide pedestal, are roughly textured and look almost lifelike. The figure of Mrs. Bethune weighs nearly 2,000 pounds and is 12 feet high. The figures of the children are nearly 9 feet tall and weigh about 1,000 pounds.

Dorothy I. Height, National President, National Council of Negro Women, Inc.

Mabel Jackson, national board member and chairperson of the "Committee of 400" for the Bethune Memorial

Nearly 18,000 people attended the dedication, including Mrs. Bethune's son, grandson, and great-grandchildren, government officials, and other notables from around the country. And several members of the Black Caucus, including Barbara Jordan, Andrew Young, Yvonne Burke, and Ronald Dellums, spoke in praise of our government for helping to make this statue possible. Then Washington's Mayor Walter Washington officially declared July 10 "Bethune Day."

On May 9, 1975, Council House, where Mrs. Bethune lived and worked from time to time, was designated as an historic landmark by the Committee on Landmarks of the National Capital.

Council House continues to this day as a living memorial. It is the location for two projects. Operation Sisters United, which gives assistance to young girls who need guidance, and COPE, which assists mothers who are heads of households.

By 1977, the National Council of Negro Women had become one of the largest and most influential organizations in the United States. Led by its inspiring president, Dorothy Height, and governed by an interracial board, its 4 million members started new projects in various parts of the country, some of them funded in part by government grants. These programs deal with the problems of hunger, housing, jobs, and health. The National Council has also cooperated in Operation Big Vote and has set up home learning centers to improve the education of poor white and ethnic children. They reached out as well to their sisters in Africa. With a one-million dollar government grant, the council has set up educational programs in three South African countries.

Another living monument, Bethune-Cookman College, continues to educate young women and men. Its lovely campus at Daytona Beach, Florida, consists of 160 acres of land. Forty acres comprise the immediate campus, with buildings and trees to give it charm. One of the striking buildings, White Hall, is named for Mr. Thomas White, a lifelong friend and benefactor of the college. At the entrance to this administration building are the words "ENTER TO LEARN," and over the exit, the words "DEPART TO SERVE." Events held in the large auditorium in White Hall have helped to mold and fashion the lives of many young people.

Sixty professors guide more than a thousand students, who come to study for a Bachelor of Arts (B.A.) degree. These students come from various parts of the South and from several foreign countries. The year 1977 produced 300 outstanding graduates, who will help to create a better world. Young people enjoy Bethune-Cookman College because it is small and friendly. Warm relationships are formed between students and faculty. In the Bethune tradition, they "enter to learn" and proudly leave "to serve."

BIBLIOGRAPHY

Adams, Russell L., *Great Negroes Past and Present.* Chicago: Afro-Am Publishing Company, 1964.

Franklin, John Hope, *From Slavery to Freedom.* New York: Alfred A. Knopf, 1964.

Holt, Rackham, *Mary McLeod Bethune.* New York: Doubleday & Company, 1964.

Hughes, Langston, *Fight for Freedom.* New York: W. W. Norton, 1962.

Katz, William L., *Eyewitness: The Negro in American History.* New York: Pitman Publishing Corporation, 1967.

Logan, Rayford W., *What the Negro Wants.* Chapel Hill: University of North Carolina Press, 1944.

Peare, Catherine Owens, *Mary McLeod Bethune.* New York: Vanguard Press, 1951.

A. Philip Randolph

2

"[We] . . . are not interested in
Negroes getting more work. Negroes
have too much work already. What we
want Negroes to get is less work and
more wages . . ."

2

A Boy
in Jacksonville

ᴢ

Aꜱᴀ ᴡᴀꜱ nine years old, old enough to know what went on around him. He watched his father walk up and down in their small house. His father had to help a man in jail.

Asa Philip Randolph was born in Crescent City, Florida, on April 15, 1889, to the Reverend and Mrs. James Randolph. Soon the family moved to Jacksonville, where Asa and his older brother, James, grew up.

It was nearly twenty-five years after the Civil War gave slaves their freedom. But Black people still had a hard time, especially in the South. Asa worried because his father worried. And he feared for the man in jail. Looking out the window, he saw crowds of white people moving in all directions. Angry men stomped around, trying to get more people to follow them. They shouted ugly names and threatened to take the man from jail. They believed he had done something wrong. These people didn't want to wait for a trial. They would punish him themselves.

"Why do they hate this man so much?" asked Asa. "Why won't they listen to his side of the story?"

"His story makes no difference to them," answered his father. "Black people are mistreated all the time. They accuse us of doing many things we have never thought of."

Asa turned to his father. "What can I do to help?" he asked anxiously. "Call your brother James. He can help us find telephone numbers," came the hurried reply. "We must act quickly, we must reach the jail first."

The Reverend Randolph, a poor Methodist minister, telephoned one man after another until he had enough brave men to guard the jail with him. While he was away, Mrs. Randolph sat up all night with a gun in her lap. She had to protect their sons and their home.

In the morning, when the angry mob moved close to the jail, they were surprised. They saw a large circle of Black men around the building. These men were afraid but knew they must stand guard, even at the risk of their lives. The white mob slowly moved back, farther and farther from the jail.

A few days later, the jailed man came to trial. It was then that Asa understood that Black people could improve their condition if they pulled together and were willing to face danger with courage. He decided then that he would work for his people when he grew up, just as his father had done. And he would try to help Black and white people get along together.

The Reverend Randolph, a tall, honest man, preached at three small churches in and around Jacksonville. Most of his followers were farmers who couldn't afford to pay for his services. Sometimes they brought him vegetables and fruit or a side of pork from their farms. Many were sharecroppers, which meant that they worked a landowner's acreage in exchange for a part of the crop. About this time, the price of cotton had dropped from a dollar a pound to five cents a pound throughout the South. White farmers became desperate for money. They didn't want to lose their homes and land.

The landowners kept the sharecropper's record of expenses and often shifted figures to keep the Black worker in debt. Even when sharecroppers knew they were being cheated, the fact that most of them had little or no schooling made it impossible for them to prove their earnings. Both white and Black sharecroppers had a difficult time, but the Black person had it harder because he had to face white sheriffs and judges if he wanted to seek justice. And he might risk his life trying to claim what was rightfully his. So, year after year, the free Black sharecropper was robbed of both his livelihood and manhood.

Some of the parishioners who attended New Hope AME (African Methodist Episcopal) Chapel were poor domestic servants or unskilled laborers who had difficulty making ends meet. When the Reverend Randolph returned home after a Sunday service, he would count a collection of nickels, dimes, and a few quarters. The only time the family could expect anything to speak of was on "Dollar Day" each year, when the church members were expected to give one dollar by rule of the AME Church.

The Randolphs were a thrifty family and planted a garden in their backyard. They also had a few chickens and a couple of hogs. Still, they were always in debt. Eventually the Reverend Randolph opened a cleaning and tailoring shop in his modest home. When he visited the sick or those in trouble, Mrs. Randolph waited on customers and did sewing. And Asa and James did odd jobs after school. First they sold newspapers, and later Asa worked in a grocery store.

The boys enjoyed swimming and games, like most children. James liked marbles and could win a game most any time. Asa's favorite game was baseball, and he played first base. When his father bought him a ball, mitt, and bat, he was the happiest boy in town.

The Randolph family liked music and literature. Some evenings they would give readings or present a play, just for their own enjoyment. And the boys often sang hymns and studied the Bible with their parents. Asa liked to read about the early leaders, like the Apostle Paul, who risked their lives to spread Christianity. Asa felt he could be just as fearless in helping to make a better life for his people. His father wanted him to become a minister, but Asa wasn't sure what path he would follow.

In the South, Black people were separated from white people in hotels, restaurants, schools, libraries, and other public places. In 1896, a few years after Asa was born, even the United States Supreme Court had declared it legal and right to have separate school systems—equal but separate. But the plan didn't work because Black people were never given the same treatment from the beginning.

Asa, a serious boy, discussed the unfair laws with his father from time to time. He felt there must be some way to change conditions. One day, the Reverend Randolph told him, "You can become a leader in changing hatred and discrimination if you want to help your people more than anything else, more than money or a fine home." As Asa stood listening, his father added, "And I believe you will."

When Asa finished grade school, he entered Cookman Institute, the first high school for Blacks in Florida. Founded in 1872, it was named for the Reverend Alfred Cookman, who donated money to have the school built. Cookman was proud of its Black and white faculty, who were better trained than many in other parts of the country. The school taught French and other languages, law, music, mathematics, and literature, along with shoemaking, printing, tailoring, and farming.

Asa was fourteen years old when he entered Cookman Institute, and James was sixteen. James was an excellent student in languages and mathematics, while Asa became the school's best student in literature and public speaking. Since they sat in the same classroom, it was easy for James to help his brother with subjects that he found difficult. The boys realized how important it was to get a good education because in that same classroom sat older men and women who hadn't had the opportunity to attend school earlier. It was at Cookman that Asa began to think and act on his own, and where his dedicated teachers saw a bright future for him.

On to New York

𝄢

AFTER HIGH SCHOOL James and Asa took whatever jobs they could find, since there was no money for college. James worked for the post office, while Asa drove a delivery wagon for a drugstore. Later, Asa worked hard, stacking logs in a lumberyard and hauling water and dirt for railroad construction. He realized that he couldn't make enough money for college this way, so he decided to make his way to New York City. He was overwhelmed by the milling crowds and the size of the big city. He thought he could find a good job there, but he was mistaken. So he took odd jobs, such as washing dishes in restaurants and cleaning stores, to support himself. Later, he worked part-time in an employment office. "Why is it so hard to find a job in the North?" he asked himself. "This is almost as bad as living in the South."

Soon Asa met a young Black student named Chandler Owen. Chandler was studying law at Columbia University in New York City and Asa, now called Phil, had just started taking night courses at the City College of New York. The two young men became friends. They spent many hours together, visiting libraries and exchanging ideas about how people live and work. They thought it was wrong for some men to be very rich while others were very poor. They believed that people had a chance to be happy only if they could earn enough to live in comfort and dignity.

After Phil found a regular job, he and Chandler opened a small employment office in Harlem, New York. They called it The Brotherhood. The two men helped to train and find work for hundreds of Blacks who came from the South. Many had come from small farms in the hope that moving to the big city would give them a better chance to get ahead.

Phil and Chandler did everything they could to help these newcomers. They used their small amount of money to keep the office open, often working late at night to get things done. Soon more men heard about The Brotherhood. Those who got jobs had to work long hours for little pay. Some returned to tell how badly they were treated.

In 1914, Philip Randolph married Lucille Green, an attractive woman who enjoyed people and parties. She had been a Virginia schoolteacher but now owned a beauty shop in New York City. She was also interested in improving working conditions and believed that everyone had the right to a good job.

Philip and Lucille Randolph both decided to become members of the Socialist Party of America. According to the Socialist theory, wealth would not be controlled by a few. Instead, the government would assume the responsibility for the employment of every able-bodied worker at acceptable wages. Those not able to work because of poor health or old age would be taken care of through government programs. A Socialist government would have free men cooperating with each other for the good of all. The Randolphs worked to spread the idea of a Socialist society that offered peace and equality to all people.

In the United States, the big labor unions helped men to get better working conditions, better pay, and shorter working hours. But Black men weren't allowed to join these unions. Philip Randolph and Owen Chandler decided to organize Black workers into their own unions. Randolph had been an elevator operator and was anxious to have these people demand a decent wage and shorter working hours. He and Chandler went from building to building, talking to the operators. In three weeks they had 600 members, who demanded eighteen dollars a week and an eight-hour working day. But soon a strike was threatened, and it became difficult to get more members, so their union folded.

Before long, a group of hotel headwaiters asked Randolph and Owen to publish a magazine for the Black waiters. The two agreed to do this and named the magazine *The Hotel Messenger*. In checking working conditions for the waiters, the publishers found that both the headwaiters and the hotel management were mistreating the waiters. For one thing, the headwaiters purchased the uniforms for the waiters, then charged them two or three times as much for them. Randolph and Chandler exposed this and other shady practices in *The Hotel Messenger*. The waiters were delighted, but the headwaiters were furious. The publishers lost their job, but they saw the power of the press. They dropped the word "Hotel" from the title and continued publishing the magazine, calling it *The Messenger*.

The Messenger

The Messenger started in 1917 in a small, dusty, third-floor room in Harlem, with credit from a Brooklyn printer. It was published monthly, and below the name was printed "The Only Radical Magazine in America." There was much for Black people to be angry about in 1917, and *The Messenger* carried an angry tone.

Woodrow Wilson, the new President from Virginia, brought the old southern separation idea to Washington with him—separate water fountains, rest rooms, and eating places in government buildings. Black federal employees were dismissed without cause. Because of this and because of increased lynchings, Black people rebelled, and race riots broke out around the country. *The Messenger* criticized Black leaders for not doing more for their people.

Randolph and Chandler also criticized the American Federation of Labor (AFL) because of its segregation practices. They said the country needed a union to include and benefit all workers. Randolph wrote, "The editors of *The Messenger* are not interested in Negroes getting more work. Negroes have too much work already. What we want Negroes to get is less work and more wages, with more leisure for study and recreation." Still, most Black workers had to beg for crumbs in the labor market. And there were other problems.

The country had just entered World War I, which carried the slogan "to make the world safe for democracy." But Americans couldn't help other people while they mistreated their own citizens. Black soldiers were insulted and beaten. They were given the worst jobs in the army. And they were organized into all-Black units, often directed by southern generals.

Philip Randolph opposed World War I because it was dishonest. He felt it dishonest for Americans to be fighting a war for democracy in Europe when democracy was denied to Black people at home in the United States. And, because he was a pacifist, he refused to serve in the army. He not only wrote fiery articles, but he made speeches all around the country. Sometimes he gave soapbox speeches on street corners in Harlem. Crowds quickly gathered when they saw this tall, commanding figure and heard his deep, convincing voice. They felt the honesty and courage of his protest. Eventually he was labeled "a dangerous radical." Once, Justice Department agents hauled Randolph off to jail for interfering with the draft. He spent a few days in jail, then was released. The case never came to trial, but Randolph was warned against continuing his activities. Still, he continued to spread the truth as he saw it. Federal agents followed him and gave him a difficult time. But Randolph would not be silenced. Also, the magazine was selling about 45,000 copies each month. Many more people were beginning to think for themselves. *The Messenger* was now receiving so many calls for help that the young editors were swamped.

Pullman Porters
Seek Help

ONE CALL CAME from the Pullman porters, who worked on trains. They carried luggage, answered questions, and did little things to make travelers comfortable. For passengers who traveled overnight, they shined their shoes and made train seats into beds. Pullman porters worked all day and nearly all night. They caught three or four hours' sleep wherever they could find a place to sit or something to lean against. A porter's pay was about sixty dollars a month. Any other money had to come from ten- or fifteen-cent tips. A few people gave larger tips, but many just said "Thank you." And these men had no paid vacations. But they were always courteous to old and young alike, and greeted passengers with a smile.

Complaints about working conditions reached the Pullman Company from time to time, but nothing was done to correct the situation. If a porter spoke too loudly or tried to organize his fellow workers, he soon found himself without a job. When the porters saw they couldn't organize by themselves, they looked for someone on the outside to help them. *The Messenger* told them who that man might be—one of the fearless editors, A. Philip Randolph.

Porters began passing copies of *The Messenger* to other porters at railroad stations from New York to California. They liked Randolph's strong words and the way he analyzed situations. A follower of the teachings of the Indian religious leader Mahatma Gandhi, he always stressed nonviolence and good will, but he believed in forceful direct action as well.

A group of New York porters asked Randolph to meet with them secretly so that their jobs wouldn't be threatened. After a long discussion of the problems and how the porters could be helped, they asked Randolph to lead them in forming a union. Philip Randolph had never been a porter and had no connection with the railroads. In fact, he wasn't sure that he had ever seen a Pullman car, much less ridden in one. He tried to think the matter through while the men waited for an answer.

The Pullman Company was one of the most powerful corporations in the United States. It had well-paid lawyers to protect its interests and was mainly interested in getting the most work for the least pay from its employees. It would take time and money to organize a union. The ten thousand porters across the country were poor, and Randolph was broke. Money from Mrs. Randolph's beauty shop helped keep *The Messenger* operating. The picture looked gloomy. What chance would the porters have against the Pullman Company? But Philip Randolph had fought for a better society ever since he was an adult, and now he would do battle with the giant Pullman Company. "I'll do it!" he told this small group of porters. "We'll organize a union."

The Brotherhood
of Sleeping Car Porters

↳

IN AUGUST 1925, Philip Randolph met with fifty porters in the Elks Hall in Harlem, New York, and organized the Brotherhood of Sleeping Car Porters. Randolph did all the talking so the Pullman Company couldn't accuse the men of organizing. But Pullman spies were busy at work, and soon the company began to question porters who had attended Brotherhood meetings. One man, Ashley Totten, was fired and became a union officer. Another, W. H. DesVerney, quit his job to work for the union, thus losing his pension. And there were others ready to make sacrifices.

Although 200 porters joined the union in the next few days, large numbers needed to be convinced that they would be doing the right thing and could survive during the difficult period ahead. Randolph and other enthusiastic union men decided to set up Brotherhood offices in other cities to increase the membership. One of the first offices was opened in Chicago, under Milton P. Webster, a porter who had left the Pullman Company several years earlier.

In 1926, in Oakland, California, Randolph met a young Pullman porter named Cottrel L. Dellums, who seemed to have leadership ability. The two men took a liking to each other immediately. While in Oakland, Randolph met with Dellums and a large group of porters. After the meeting, he could see that the men feared for their jobs and families. Then Dellums stood and faced the men, saying, "I know you're worried, but your job is hard, with long hours and low pay. And on top of this, you've got a mean boss man. You have to take a stand for what you believe is fair sometime, and it might as well be now." Glancing around the room, he added, "Let's organize! What do we have to lose?"

After a heated discussion, the men agreed to fight for their rights. But when word got around about the meeting, Dellums lost his job. He began working as leader of the porters on the West Coast, and his efforts in the long struggle for union recognition became invaluable.

Randolph saw how men could be won over and how he might be able to form a national organization. On his return to New York, he met with church and lodge people, asking support for Black workers. He said that right after the Civil War, in 1867, when the Pullman Company introduced the sleeping car, Black men were glad to get any job because they had been forced under slavery to work without pay for so long. But times had changed, and twenty-five or thirty cents an hour was no money at all for a man. Randolph visited porters in their homes and in their club groups. He held meetings in cities around the country and organized local unions at the same time. There was no time to lose because nearly 10,000 porters had not yet joined the union.

In 1928, Randolph organized a Wall Street demonstration in New York City. He consulted his friend, C. L. Dellums, in working out the plans. The Pullman porters didn't march, but their many friends walked for them. They carried signs reading "Jobs for All" and "We Want Fair Working Conditions." Members of the Women's Auxiliary of the Brotherhood marched and supported their men all the way. Most of the marchers were Black and white women. This demonstration caused much excitement because it was unusual at that time to see women in a labor march.

The Brotherhood:
a National Organization

𝕫

IN SEPTEMBER 1929, Philip Randolph called about fifty retired and discharged porters together in Chicago, Illinois. They came from different cities, representing local unions. He told them, "We want unions around the country to unite. Regular passenger service on airplanes is just beginning. But the American people depend on the railroads, and our Black railroad workers are carrying the heavy burden. Progress must come, even if it means peaceful revolution."

The men were inspired by his talk. Before the meeting closed, the Brotherhood of Sleeping Car Porters became a national organization. With great cheers, the men elected Philip Randolph president.

Randolph set up labor conferences and workshops from coast to coast to make sure the men realized the importance of the organization. A collection was taken after each conference so that Randolph could buy a ticket to the next city. The country was divided into seven zones, with a leader over each zone. And members paid one dollar a month in dues to cover expenses. Men began signing up all over the country. Soon they had more than 6,000 union porters.

Whenever possible, whether on the road or at home, Philip Randolph read books and attended lectures and plays. And he enjoyed good radio programs. He could not pass a magazine stand without stopping. He had a keen sense of humor and always looked for cartoons that said something important in a clever way. He also had many discussions with people of different races and beliefs. In this way, he continued to be prepared in his role as a leader.

The main office of the Brotherhood was in *The Messenger*'s two-room office on Seventh Avenue in New York. Under the title on the magazine was printed, "The Official Organ of the Brotherhood of Sleeping Car Porters." Now that "the Brotherhood" and *"The Messenger"* were linked, Philip Randolph was ready to present the long list of porter complaints to the Pullman Company and to the public. The public must be persuaded to understand and give support to the struggle.

The Long, Hard Fight

FIRST, the porters wanted the Pullman Company to recognize their union, the Brotherhood of Sleeping Car Porters. They also wanted the company to sign a contract with them and agree on salaries, working conditions, and a decent pension. Most porters worked one hundred hours a month for sixty dollars. This money didn't include overtime work, preparing cars before trips, or cleaning them up afterward. It didn't include a porter's meals, his uniform, or the brushes and polishes he used to clean passengers' shoes. And if a towel, sheet, or blanket was missing at the end of a trip, the porter was held responsible and had to pay for the item. The union demanded $150 a month and shorter working hours.

The Pullman Company gave porters a pension of eighteen dollars a month after they had worked twenty years and had reached seventy years of age. But it claimed the right to cancel the pension at any time without reason. Some pensions were stopped abruptly when the company suspected union activity.

The Pullman Company refused to meet with Randolph and other Brotherhood officials. And it refused to recognize the union. Soon the company offered a stock-purchase plan and an 8 percent increase in wages, thinking this would satisfy the porters. Randolph denounced these schemes and asked the men to stand firm, even though the company had been firing hundreds of porters and replacing them with men from the Philippines. He continued his speeches and articles while the Pullman Company called him an outside agitator and a dangerous leader.

In 1928, when the situation had become unbearable, Randolph had sought help from the National Board of Mediation, but the Pullman Company wouldn't cooperate. Then he and other Black leaders called upon President Coolidge to let him know of a pending strike by the porters, since they hadn't been able to improve their situation in any other way. Coolidge listened politely but promised nothing. Now, in 1929, Randolph met with William Green of the American Federation of Labor (AFL). Randolph had been harsh in his criticism of the AFL because most of its local unions had refused to accept Black workers. But now he needed the AFL's help: The strike date had already been set, and the Brotherhood needed the support of other unions to make the strike effective.

William Green and A. Philip Randolph discussed the matter for a long time. Green wanted to help, but he convinced Randolph that it would be unwise to stage a strike at that time. The country was in the middle of the Great Depression, and millions of people were out of work and hungry. A year earlier would have been risky, but now a strike by Black workers would surely fail. Randolph stiffened in his chair. The president of the powerful AFL was right.

Randolph faced his men with a heavy heart when he announced postponement of the strike. The men became discouraged because they knew that "postponement" meant no strike at all. In a few short months, the union membership of more than 7,000 dwindled to less than 3,000. The Brotherhood owed rent money, and telephone and electricity services were shut off because there was no money to pay bills. Even *The Messenger* had to close its doors. Some union officials took on part-time jobs, while others went without salary. Randolph, who had refused to accept any salary in the beginning and only enough to live on later, gave up all his income from the union.

The Pullman Company saw this as the time to strike a blow. Randolph received a letter from a man known to have connections with the Pullman Company. The envelope held a check for $10,000. The letter read, "You have done all anyone could be expected to do. Now that the cause is lost, please accept this check as a reward and take a trip to Europe." Randolph was shocked and angry. "Do they really think they can buy me?" he wondered. How could he betray the brothers who had gone into debt, gone hungry, and lost their pensions? "I will not take Pullman gold. The Pullman Company thinks it can buy the Brotherhood, but they are wrong."

When the porters learned of the incident, they knew they had to support a man like this, a man they could trust. They knew he was weary and without money. Still he stood firm and proved that the cause meant more to him than money. A. Philip Randolph was indeed their "Chief." Porters returned to the union in large numbers, with a new spirit and determination. Soon two grants came from the Garland Fund, which helped to rebuild the organization. And Randolph, who had been able to replace *The Messenger* with a newspaper called *The Black Worker*—he chose the name because he said it was good to be Black and be a worker—was pleading the cause of labor unions for all workers. Working people had always been the backbone of the country.

In 1934, sleeping car porters were included in the Railway Labor Act of 1926, which was supposed to protect the right of railroad workers to organize. Before this time, no one seemed to be able to force Pullman to deal with the Brotherhood. Now the National Mediation Board took a vote of the porters to see who they wanted to represent them. The vote was overwhelmingly in favor of the Brotherhood. The Pullman Company was now required to negotiate and recognize the Brotherhood as a legitimate union. But the company refused to go down to defeat without one more try.

One day, Randolph and William Bowe, a porter official, visited the home of a man they thought was a company spy. Another man was there. While Bowe stood in an adjoining room, this man offered Randolph a check and told him to fill in the amount. The Pullman Company wanted him to leave the Brotherhood. Bowe was surprised at what he overheard. And Randolph was angry all over again. Earlier, he had sent back the first check Pullman had given him. Now he had to remind the company that it was dealing with a new Negro who could not be turned around.

William Green, the president of the AFL, had followed the struggle of the Brotherhood of Sleeping Car Porters against the powerful Pullman Company. He couldn't help but admire the determined leadership of Philip Randolph and the many sacrifices of the porters. In 1935, Mr. Green gave the Brotherhood assistance in becoming a full member union of the American Federation of Labor. Shortly after their 1935 convention, the industrial unions (made up of many kinds of workers) left the AFL and formed their own organization, called the Congress of Industrial Organizations (CIO). This gave thousands of Black workers a chance to become unionized. Later the two organizations merged, becoming the AFL-CIO.

Even with recognition of the Brotherhood by the AFL and the formation of the CIO, the Pullman Company was reluctant to meet with union officials. But after many delays, negotiations finally started in 1935. They dragged on for two years. In 1937, twelve years after the Brotherhood was organized, the Pullman Company officials signed a contract with the Brotherhood of Sleeping Car Porters, the first Black union in the United States.

The Pullman official who signed the contract shook Randolph's hand and said, "The Pullman Company will keep its part of the agreement. There will always be problems, but now we have a means of settling them." Randolph smiled and said, "And we, too, will honor the agreement."

The Black union members received close to 2 million dollars in wage increases and a sixty-hour working week. Also, the amount of travel was reduced from 11,000 miles a month to 7,000 miles. The long, hard fight was over. The Black worker, led by a Black leader, had proved that he could stand tall and bargain for himself. Celebrations took place all over the country. And A. Philip Randolph had become, almost overnight, the most popular labor leader in the United States.

Black Workers and Soldiers in World War II

🗲

IN 1939, at the beginning of World War II, there were 4,000 more porters serving train passengers than in peacetime. With so many people moving about, there were many problems. Philip Randolph traveled around the country, settling disputes and encouraging the men. He always reminded them that they represented their race and their country. Sometimes he went to trouble spots when he was so weary that he could hardly stay awake. But when they needed him, he went. He also gave advice and help when calls came from people doing other kinds of work. If a situation became extremely difficult, he called upon the President of the United States for action.

When World War II began, there were few openings for Black men and women in defense industries. Randolph, accompanied by Walter White of the NAACP (National Association for the Advancement of Colored People) and T. Arnold Hill of the National Urban League, met with President Franklin D. Roosevelt. This committee wanted to make sure that Black men and women would be given the same kind of defense jobs as other Americans. President Roosevelt listened to the men but gave them no assurance that he would take care of the matter. When the President was slow to act, Randolph threatened to march 100,000 Black people to Washington in nonviolent protest. Word was spread by word of mouth, speeches, and articles. And the masses were making preparations to move when the "Chief" gave the word.

"Call off the march!" he was told. "Progress will come. Everything will work out all right." But this was not enough for Philip Randolph. He refused to call off the march until President Roosevelt issued Executive Order 8802 on June 25, 1941, just five days before the march was to take place. This order said: "There shall be no discrimination in the employment of workers in defense industries or government because of race, creed, color, or national origin."

The President then formed the FEPC (Fair Employment Practices Committee) to check on conditions in defense plants around the country and to report any discrimination. This was important because it meant that some men and women were sure of a real job for the first time in their lives. And others were now able to advance from unskilled to skilled labor. The earnings of Black people increased by billions of dollars because of this order. Another big gain in preparing for the march was that both educated and uneducated Blacks had a chance to participate. They all had a right to be proud when the march could be called off. Randolph was hailed throughout the country. He received the coveted Spingarn Medal from the NAACP and an honorary degree from Howard University, and he was named to the Schomburg Collection Honor Roll.

The discrimination-in-labor battle had been won, but Blacks still faced the same conditions in the United States Army. Black men had fought bravely in the Revolutionary War, the War of 1812, the Civil War, and World War I. Thousands hurried to enlist each time there was an emergency, and many won medals for bravery. During World War II, Randolph risked going to prison because of his talks with Black and white soldiers. He urged them not to fight if they had to live in separate camps and fight in separate units. He told them to go to jail first. He said, "You are both Americans, fighting the same war for the same country. Why shouldn't you live and fight together?"

After the war, Randolph continued his fight for a united American army because there were still thousands of men in separate camps in the United States and in Europe. He called upon President Truman several times, until the President became angry. But after twenty Black soldiers went to jail and hundreds more refused to fight if called upon, President Truman issued Executive Order 9981 on July 26, 1948. The order said: "There shall be equality of treatment and opportunity for all persons in the armed services without regard to race, color, religion, or national origin." Soon a committee was set up to see that the order was enforced. Now Black and white servicemen could live and fight together for their country. They got along well and performed many tasks better than when they were in separate camps.

A Leader in the AFL-CIO

⚡

BACK IN 1925, while Randolph was trying desperately to organize Black workers, he was highly critical of the white labor unions for excluding Blacks. In 1926, William Green, president of the American Federation of Labor, invited Randolph to attend the AFL convention as an observer. As Randolph sat listening, he saw that the racial issue seemed to be of little importance to the members. He became convinced, there and then, that he might be able to wage a stronger fight for equality within this big, white union. A few years later, Randolph became one of the first Black men to join the powerful AFL. Gradually other Blacks were admitted.

The AFL (comprised of international unions) had endorsed a policy of nondiscrimination, but it continued to be difficult for the international unions to control their local unions. In the South, many local units refused to accept the national ruling and threatened to withdraw if any pressure was put upon them. And some unions used various means to keep Black workers out. From the time of Randolph's entrance in the AFL, he spoke out at meetings, trying to show members how much stronger the organization would be if it included all workers, which was supposed to be a right of people living in a democracy.

After the AFL and CIO merged, Randolph and George Meany, president of the AFL-CIO, discussed the matter of Black workers many times. They argued in open meetings because Meany thought Randolph wanted to move too fast in admitting Black workers. He thought it might cause trouble within the union. But Randolph, always a gentleman, always modest and polite, continued, in a dignified manner, to fight for what he felt was right. During the 1950's, because so many Black people were still not protected by unions, Randolph helped to organize Black teachers, farm workers, and people in various trades. Then he formed the Negro American Labor Council to strengthen these unions.

Philip Randolph became so forceful that white union leaders had to admire and respect him. In 1957, he became vice-president of the AFL-CIO, the largest of all labor organizations. And in 1960, the Negro American Labor Council reported that there were one and a half million Black union members.

From the time Philip Randolph was a young man, he always seemed to know when it was time to act. He had proved it on many occasions, especially with the Pullman Company and with the two executive orders. Now it was time to act again, because after years of struggle, millions of Black citizens still needed decent jobs. And they needed to be respected like other Americans.

Randolph proposed a massive, orderly march on Washington to keep up the pressure for fair treatment of minorities. Several white leaders and government officials were opposed to it. But Dr. Martin Luther King, Jr. was interested. So were Roy Wilkins (NAACP), Whitney Young (Urban League), Dorothy Height (NCNW), and others. It was agreed that only one man could get the cooperation of all the leaders—A. Philip Randolph. Soon the "Chief" formed an interracial committee to organize the March on Washington. And he selected civil rights activist Bayard Rustin to coordinate and direct the March.

The March on Washington

𝓏

On August 28, 1963, more than 250,000 Black and white Americans marched to the nation's capital for "Jobs and Freedom." Young white couples came with their children, while others leaned on canes as they moved along. Some carried signs reading "March for Jobs for All Now" and "First-Class Citizenship Now." Many covered their heads as protection from the scorching sun. But these thousands kept marching, making this the biggest and most orderly protest in American history.

After the opening remarks, Randolph said, "The March on Washington is not the climax of our struggle but a new beginning, not only for the Negro but for all Americans who thirst for freedom and a better life." And after Dr. Martin Luther King, Jr. gave his "I Have a Dream" speech, Randolph stood by the Lincoln Memorial with his long-time friend and assistant, Bayard Rustin, at his side. With tears streaming down his face, he watched the huge crowds turn to go home. What a wonderful day! People had come from all over. They had walked and stood in the hot sun to say they wanted a better life for everyone.

President John F. Kennedy asked for laws to make sure that all Americans would be treated fairly. The next year, President Lyndon B. Johnson signed the Civil Rights Act of 1964, which provided for basic rights for all citizens.

A. Philip Randolph with Dr. Ralph Bunche and William Green at a meeting in New York City, 1950

International Convention of the Brotherhood of Sleeping Car Porters, Los Angeles, 1953; C. L. Dellums at the microphone, A. Philip Randolph to his right

Prayer pilgrimage to Washington, D.C., 1957: (*left to right*) Roy Wilkins,
A. Philip Randolph, Rev. Thomas Kilgore, Dr. Martin Luther King, Jr.

Harlem street rally, 1958: (*left to right*) Jackie Robinson,
A. Philip Randolph, Adam Clayton Powell, Jr.

Bayard Rustin and A. Philip Randolph at Mr. Randolph's home,
New York City, 1969

Arthur M. Powell, member of *A. Philip Randolph Leaders of Tomorrow*,
saluting Mr. Randolph at his eightieth birthday party at the Waldorf Astoria,
New York City, May 6, 1969

A. Philip Randolph with Roy Wilkins at Mr. Randolph's eightieth birthday party, the Waldorf Astoria, New York City, May 6, 1969

Philip Randolph had worked for nonviolent change and for harmony among the races. Now everyone wanted to honor him. He received awards from the Teachers' Guild, the Newspaper Guild, and the League for Industrial Democracy. In 1964 came perhaps the greatest honor of his life, when the Presidential Medal of Freedom was presented to him by President Lyndon B. Johnson. This gold medal represents the highest award that can be given to any American citizen for service to mankind. And in 1965, an area in Harlem, New York, was officially named "A. Philip Randolph Square" in his honor.

Bayard Rustin, a man who had been helping his people for a long time, told why Mr. Randolph deserved such a high honor. He said, "He has never acted selfishly and I, for one, know of the time when he would go for weeks with nothing to eat but beans. Often, when he was working with the union, he would leave New York with only enough money for a one-way ticket and would have to remain in Chicago until he could raise enough money to come back home. He's a beautiful human being, a magnificent man."

The A. Philip Randolph Institute

🖎

In 1965, Randolph started the A. Philip Randolph Institute in New York City to study poverty and help correct injustice among the races. Bayard Rustin, who is now president of the institute, was named its director. Much regard and great respect was shown Randolph when the AFL-CIO gave $30,000 to assist the institute with its program. Since then, local unions throughout the country and the national office have made substantial contributions each year. And other groups donate money as well.

With Randolph's experience and good judgment, the institute helps to settle disputes and to guide young people and new movements. With local units in various cities, it gives important information to Black people from time to time. And it sends workers around the country to assist with voter registration and to plan political campaigns. In the program "Outreach," the institute helps Blacks and other minorities find jobs in the construction and building trades.

An important plan, called "Freedom Budget for All Americans," was proposed by Randolph at the 1965 White House Conference on Civil Rights. It was worked out at the institute and presented to the public. By training people and creating worthwhile jobs with tax money collected from American citizens, it would eliminate poverty in ten years. Then everyone could live as a respected human being. The plan is still in progress.

Philip Randolph has been interested in the welfare of people everywhere. On two occasions, the AFL-CIO sent him around the world to organize and to improve labor unions. As he talked with people of different races, he found that they wanted better working conditions and a happier life for all. Since that time, a great deal of money for the institute has come from international unions.

In 1968, Randolph retired as president of the Brotherhood of Sleeping Car Porters but returned to serve as a board member. C. L. Dellums, who had helped organize the Brotherhood on the West Coast and who had worked steadily with Randolph through the years, then became Brotherhood president.

Early in 1969, Randolph celebrated his eightieth birthday. His many friends and well-wishers decided to celebrate the occasion with a dinner at the Waldorf-Astoria in New York City. It was a grand evening. People from all walks of life came to pay tribute to this dedicated man who, years earlier, had been called "the most dangerous Negro in America" because he was determined to change and improve society. Labor and church leaders, congressmen, judges, and representatives from all kinds of clubs and unions were in attendance. George Meany, C. L. Dellums, Carl Rowan, Whitney Young, Roy Wilkins, and Nelson Rockefeller were among those giving special praise. Randolph acknowledged their tributes with the voice and the modest manner that was his alone. What a glorious birthday party!

Randolph resigned as a vice-president of the AFL-CIO in 1974. Because of his health, he had been advised not to travel so much. C. L. Dellums then became a vice-president of the AFL-CIO. But Randolph continued to give advice and assistance to individuals and groups, and to guide the work of the institute.

In 1976, a Bicentennial tribute was given in honor of Philip Randolph. Congratulations streamed in from local units of the institute and from friends everywhere. A. Philip Randolph had indeed proved himself to be a fearless Black leader, an outstanding American and world citizen. All hail the Chief!

BIBLIOGRAPHY

Adams, Russell L., *Great Negroes Past and Present.* Chicago: Afro-Am Publishing Company, 1964.

Anderson, Jervis, *A. Philip Randolph.* New York: Harcourt Brace Jovanovich, 1972.

Franklin, John Hope, *Black Americans.* New York: Time-Life Books, 1973.

Franklin, John Hope, *From Slavery to Freedom.* New York: Alfred A. Knopf, 1964.

Hughes, Langston, *Fight for Freedom.* New York: W. W. Norton, 1962.

Katz, William L., *Eyewitness: The Negro in American History.* New York: Pitman Publishing Corporation, 1967.

Thomas, Norman, *What Are the Answers?* New York: Ives Washburn, 1970.

Martin Luther King, Jr.

"We've got some difficult days ahead. But it really doesn't matter with me now, because I've been to the mountaintop. And I've seen the Promised Land. I may not get there with you. But I want you to know tonight that we as a people will get to the Promised Land!"

Growing Up in the South

👉

DESPITE SEGREGATION and racial troubles in the South, the boyhood of Martin Luther King, Jr. was more tolerable than that experienced by thousands of other Black children. His father was a minister and his mother a teacher. Born in Atlanta on January 15, 1929, Martin was blessed with loving and deeply religious parents, a comfortable home, an older sister, Christine, and a younger brother, Alfred Daniel. They all enjoyed good times together.

Martin made friends easily at school and was considered a peacemaker when arguments arose. He liked to wrestle and would take on any of the boys. He spent a great deal of time reading, and on Sundays he listened intently as his father preached his sermon about people loving one another.

At Washington High School, Martin became an outstanding athlete. He enjoyed basketball and was a fullback on the football team. He dressed well, and because he was a good dancer, the girls enjoyed his company. But he continued to study hard and was able to skip two grades. He also seemed to have the gift of oratory and often practiced his talks in front of a mirror. His choice of words and his manner of expressing himself won him a speaking contest in Atlanta.

Soon Martin had a chance to go to Valdosta, Georgia, to participate in the state finals of the Elks' oratorical contest. He traveled with his teacher, and was happy and proud when he won the second-place prize. On the trip home, they took seats near the front of the bus because there were no seats in the Negro section. When the bus made a village stop, some white passengers boarded the bus. The driver gave Martin and his teacher an angry look and snapped, "Move back!" His teacher moved back and stood. But Martin remained seated. Hadn't he paid the same fare as the other passengers? Wasn't he conducting himself as he should? Why should he be forced to move back because he was Black?

Martin knew that Black people were supposed to sit in the rear. Still he sat where he was. His teacher pleaded with him to move, while the angry driver yelled ugly words at him. Finally, when his teacher tugged at his arm and said, "Please, Martin," he moved. Steadying himself by holding on to the bus strap, he stood all the way back to Atlanta, a distance of nearly one hundred miles.

Standing there, this slim brown boy thought of his father fighting unfair laws at every turn—how he had refused to ride segregated buses and had demanded to be called "man" instead of "boy." And he could hear his mother's voice saying, "Remember, you are as smart and as good as anyone." Gazing straight ahead, he made a promise to himself. He would work to help people act like brothers, no matter what happened.

Martin was only fifteen when he enrolled at Morehouse College in Atlanta. A number of strong-minded Black men had studied at Morehouse, including his father and grandfather. Entering college at so young an age seemed to frighten him a little. He did his work well but showed no signs of becoming a leader.

Martin's only prank, along with a classmate, was to drink from water fountains marked "White." But he was fearless in time of trouble. When a college friend was about to be shot by a white man during a heated argument, young Martin jumped to his friend's side, defying the white man and his gun.

With Black people jailed on the slightest charge and with injustice in the courts, Martin thought of studying law so he could defend his people. Then he thought of the sick and dying, who often received no care. A doctor could help so many people. He might study medicine. Then he remembered his father saying that a minister must not only talk of love, but must work in the community. A minister could see all the trouble a family had and guide them out of their despair.

At seventeen, after two years of college, Martin preached his first sermon at his father's church. Large numbers of people came to hear him. They told him they were pleased with his speech. He became assistant pastor at Ebenezer Baptist Church and realized this was the course he would follow.

Preparing for Leadership

🖎

DURING THE summer months, Martin unloaded trucks at a mattress factory. And he loaded trains and cleaned stores. These jobs didn't pay much, but Martin was rubbing shoulders with Black men. His friendly and encouraging manner helped them to forget their hardships for a while.

Martin graduated from Morehouse College in 1948. The following September, he enrolled at Crozer Theological Seminary in Chester, Pennsylvania, for a three-year course in the ministry. All his life he had attended Black schools. At Crozer, with no Jim Crow laws, Black and white students mingled and studied together. Martin made so many friends that he was soon elected class president.

While at Crozer, Martin began a serious study of peace movements. He wanted to know how other poor people had freed themselves from unfair treatment. He read about the great Hindu leader, Mahatma Gandhi. For years, Gandhi used peaceful methods to help the poor people of India free themselves from British rule. Gandhi fasted. And he was jailed many times for breaking unfair laws. His followers used marches and boycotts to change conditions. When they were arrested, they went to jail without fighting.

In 1951, Martin graduated from Crozer Theological Seminary. He won the important Plafker Award. He also received a $1,200 scholarship, which he used for further study at Boston University in Massachusetts.

In Boston, Martin studied Communism, which said there should be only one class of people, not rich and poor. But he didn't accept Communism because it had no place for God and because it made the government more important than the people. Sometimes small groups of college students would meet with Martin to discuss the problems of poor Black people in the United States.

In 1951, a friend introduced Martin to Coretta Scott, a beautiful young student from Alabama. She had come to Boston to study and become a concert singer. At first, she wasn't interested in meeting a minister. But soon she and Martin became good friends and fell in love. In 1953, they were married in the garden of Coretta's Alabama home by Martin's father, the Reverend Martin Luther King, Sr.

When Martin and Coretta finished their studies in Boston, they had to make important decisions. Martin had received a degree that gave him the title of Doctor. He had been offered positions by several churches, some in the North. And what about Coretta's singing career? The young minister and his wife discussed their choices for days and weeks.

Coretta decided that she loved Martin enough to give up her concert plans. And Martin, who had been talking about a better life for Black people, had to ask himself, "Do I really care enough to go where I'm needed?" He thought back to the time he stood on a bus for a hundred-mile ride rather than sit in the back. And he knew that Coretta shared his ideas. So he accepted a position in the South, where life was hardest for Black people.

Dr. King became minister of the Dexter Avenue Baptist Church in Montgomery, Alabama. He prepared his sermons carefully, and this brought new members to the church. He visited the sick and the lonely. He also worked with organizations in the community for better jobs and living conditions. The Black people of Montgomery began to look up to him as a new leader. Coretta worked at his side and sang in the church choir.

Montgomery, like Atlanta, had Jim Crow laws—separate schools, churches, restaurants, theaters, and taxis. On city buses, Black people were often insulted by the bus drivers. All passengers entered at the front to pay their fares. The bus driver then ordered Black people to walk around and climb back on, to sit in the rear. When whites didn't have seats, Black passengers had to stand, no matter how tired they were. The fact that they had paid the same fare and conducted themselves well made no difference.

The Bus Boycott

ℤ

ON DECEMBER 1, 1955, Rosa Parks, a quiet Black woman, started a revolution in the South. She boarded a bus in Montgomery, paid her fare, and sat down. Soon more white people got on, but there were no seats for them. The bus driver told Mrs. Parks to give her seat to a white woman. Rosa Parks didn't get up. She had worked all day in a department store and was tired. Her feet hurt. And she hurt all over because she wasn't treated with respect.

The bus driver yelled at her, telling her to stand or face arrest. Still Mrs. Parks remained seated. The bus driver called a policeman, who took her to the police station, where she was fingerprinted and held in jail.

The bad news spread like a blazing fire. Black citizens of Montgomery were enraged. A group of Black women leaders called for a bus boycott. A Black leader, Mr. E. D. Nixon, talked with Mrs. Parks, who said, "Just having paid for a seat and riding for only a couple of blocks and then having to stand was too much."

Mr. Nixon called Dr. Martin Luther King, Jr. and another young minister, the Reverend Ralph Abernathy. They decided to call for a boycott of the city buses for one day to protest the arrest of Mrs. Parks. Although thousands of Black people in Montgomery depended on buses to get to and from work, they were ready for action. Telephones rang day and night. A leaflet was circulated, which said:

> Another Negro has been arrested and put in jail because she refused to give up her bus seat.
>
> Don't ride the buses to work, to town, to school, or anywhere on Monday, December 5. If you work, take a cab, or share a ride, or walk.
>
> Come to a mass meeting Monday night at 7 o'clock at the Holt Street Baptist Church.

Dr. and Mrs. King awakened early the morning of the boycott. They had coffee, then moved about quietly so they wouldn't wake their infant daughter, Yolanda Denise. Mrs. King stood by the window. Suddenly she called, "Martin, come quick! The buses are rolling, and there are no Black riders. The buses are nearly empty!" Dr. King rushed to her side. Then came an idea. If necessary, why not extend the boycott until the company went broke?

That night, thousands of Black people crowded at the church for the meeting. What should they do now? Would the boycott continue? After the arrest of Mrs. Parks, an organization called the Montgomery Improvement Association was formed, and Dr. King was elected president.

Dr. King asked the people to stay off the buses until they received better treatment. And he urged them to make it a peaceful protest. Were they ready to sacrifice? When the vote was taken, people jumped to their feet and cheered. The bus boycott would continue! Bayard Rustin, a Black civil rights organizer, assisted in planning the protest. This marked the biggest revolt by Black people in the United States.

These Montgomery citizens drove cars, rode taxis, hitched rides, and rode mules. Soon car pools were organized. The leaders held weekly meetings, during which the people sang and prayed. Then they took turns giving instructions in nonviolence—if somebody calls you a name, don't listen; if somebody slaps your face or kicks you, don't strike back. Dr. King reminded them of Booker T. Washington's words, "Let no man pull you so low as to make you hate him."

Day after day, thousands of Black people looked at nearly empty buses while they walked in the rain and against cold winds. Young and old walked until their shoes were worn down and their feet were sore. Before the boycott more than 17,000 Black people rode the buses twice a day. Now only a handful continued to travel by bus. Insults and heckling continued, but each week the prayers, songs, and "pep" talks gave the people courage to carry on until the next meeting.

The white people of Montgomery wanted the boycott ended. They didn't want to ride buses while there was trouble, so they stayed home or used other means of transportation. As time passed, fewer and fewer whites rode the buses. The large stores were losing customers and money, and so was the bus company.

Soon the Black leaders met with bus company and city officials. Dr. King and his committee wanted Black passengers to be able to sit where they wanted to, the drivers to be courteous, and some Black bus drivers hired. But the talks didn't settle anything, and the boycott went on. Now the white officials became furious. The police chief told his officiers to get tough with the Blacks. And they did!

First, they arrested Dr. King, accusing him of driving too fast. Dr. King knew he hadn't broken the law, but he was forced to go to jail. Black people surrounded the jail in such numbers that the jailer became fearful. The police chief quickly set Dr. King free.

Another time, Dr. King was speaking at a meeting when he received word that a bomb had been thrown at his house. Returning home, he saw that a crowd had gathered and that the explosion had blown a big hole in the porch and shattered some windows. He rushed inside to make sure his family was safe. Then the mayor, police chief, and several white reporters arrived. And more than a thousand Blacks surrounded the house. Some wanted to fight it out with the whites.

Dr. King stood on his front steps and tried to quiet the crowd, asking those who had knives or guns to take them home. He said, "We must love our white brothers, no matter what they do. Remember, if I am stopped, this movement will not stop, because God is with the movement." By this time, photographers had arrived and were flashing pictures for all the world to see. Dr. Martin Luther King, Jr. had become a national leader.

Weeks stretched into months. Buses, with angry-faced drivers, rolled along, nearly empty. Newspapers, as well as radio and television, kept the people informed. Thousands of white people in the North sent money to help the Blacks in their struggle. And money came from as far away as Tokyo and Singapore.

During this time, the King family received several telephone threats on their lives. There were hateful letters, too. At one point, Dr. King nearly gave up. How could he protect his family against such threats? Late one night, after an upsetting call, he turned to God for strength and courage, and he was able to go on.

In March 1956, the city officials had the boycott leaders arrested for stopping the bus company's business. Dr. King was found guilty and fined $500. When he and Coretta left court, he was smiling because he knew his only crime was trying to help his people. The fight would go on until they won!

In November 1956, white leaders in Montgomery asked the judge to declare the Black car pool unlawful because they said it was unfair to the bus company. Dr. King began to worry. This was a serious charge. The case had been appealed to the Supreme Court, but no decision had come.

Dr. King sat in the courtroom, thinking, wondering,

when a reporter slipped a note into his hand. It said the United States Supreme Court had ruled that Jim Crow buses were against the law. Black people had won the fight after boycotting the Montgomery buses for 381 days after the one-day boycott.

On December 20, 1956, the Supreme Court order arrived in Montgomery. Now the city buses were integrated. Early the next morning, Dr. King and three of his assistants boarded the bus near his home. The driver smiled and said, "I believe you are the Reverend King?"

"Yes, I am," Dr. King answered.

"We are glad to have you this morning," said the driver.

Dr. King took a seat near the front of the bus. The Reverend Smiley, a white minister and friend, sat beside him. The bus rolled down the street and across town. Now Jim Crow buses were gone from Montgomery forever!

But white racists became angrier. They fired on buses at night, bombed three churches, and damaged the homes of Black leaders. A woman was shot, and a Black girl was beaten. These whites even threatened to hang a Supreme Court justice. Dr. King became worried. He didn't want to see blood shed by anyone. But his followers convinced him that they were all in the fight together and that they needed his leadership.

Why couldn't all unfair laws be wiped out in the South? Dr. King met with leaders in Atlanta, and they organized a new group called the Southern Christian Leadership Conference, or SCLC. The organizers elected Martin Luther King, Jr. president. Now he would have even less time with his family.

Dr. King held meetings in various cities, where he explained the method of nonviolence to new groups. He encouraged the people to break unfair laws and to go to jail quietly when arrested. "Have no fear," he told them. "We can win!"

The Right to Vote

𝔎

ONE OF THE WORST forms of injustice was "the vote." Black people couldn't improve their condition if they couldn't elect men to office who believed in fair laws. Black people had to pay taxes, but rules were made to keep them from voting. Sometimes they were required to pay a tax or take a test that few white voters could have passed.

SCLC leaders rolled up their sleeves and went to work. Dr. King directed young people in voter registration. He was busier than ever because he was writing a book and still serving as minister of Dexter Avenue Baptist Church. Soon he gave up his post and moved to Atlanta, where he could serve as assistant in his father's church. The Kings had a warm feeling for Montgomery because of the historic bus boycott and because Yolanda Denise and Martin Luther King III had been born there. As they joined hands with the church members for a farewell hymn, tears came to their eyes.

Sit-Ins
and Freedom Rides
ぇ

IN FEBRUARY 1959, a group of Black teenagers tested Jim Crow at a Woolworth store in Greensboro, North Carolina. They sat at a lunch counter and waited to be served. Whites moved away from them, calling them ugly names. The waitress refused to serve them. A policeman came and arrested them. The next day more Black students sat at the counter, waiting to be served. Arrests went on for days and weeks. Sometimes the teenagers were insulted. Often they were followed and beaten by angry white youths. The police were rough with them. But they continued to sit at lunch counters until some of the stores began to serve them. Now these students could see an end to Jim Crow in Greensboro.

Soon marches and "sit-ins" were started in other cities. Dr. King led many of the marches with his good friend, the Reverend Ralph Abernathy. When the police stopped them, Dr. King was usually the first to be taken to jail. They thought that if they removed the leader, perhaps his followers would give up. But this was not the case. Sometimes forty or fifty people were jailed for quietly protesting an unfair law. When the marchers stopped to pray, they often looked up to see guns or clubs near their heads, while white bystanders called them ugly names.

Many white people, including many college students from the North, East, and West, joined the marchers.

They knew America could not be a great country while it mistreated its Black citizens. These white people were beaten and jailed, too. Some had to hide or leave town to keep from being killed.

Sometimes the marchers sat down to rest and sing freedom songs. A favorite song went something like this:

> We are not afraid, we are not afraid,
> We are not afraid today.
> Oh, deep in my heart, I do believe
> We shall overcome someday.
> Black and white together, Black and white together,
> We shall overcome someday.
> Oh, deep in my heart, I do believe
> We shall overcome someday.

After the "vote" and the sit-ins came the Freedom Rides. Black and some white students from all over the country decided to ride the buses that traveled from one state to another. This was a dangerous thing to try, but they were determined to change conditions. In May 1961, thirteen freedom riders left Washington, D.C., on two Greyhound buses going south. The students sat in front seats, used "white" waiting rooms at bus stops, drank from "white" drinking fountains and sat at lunch counters marked "Whites Only."

The news spread with whirlwind speed. When the riders reached Alabama, angry whites cut the tires on the first bus and followed it out of town. When the tires went flat, they set fire to the bus and started to beat the riders with fists, metal pipes, and baseball bats. More freedom riders took bus trips, only to be attacked by whites who said, "Don't try it again."

Dr. King spoke to a group of battered freedom riders in a Montgomery Church. Outside, angry voices could be heard. Rocks and bottles were slammed against the side of the church. Threats to kill the riders came sailing through the air. The mob tried to break in. Dr. King, fearful for the young people, hurriedly placed a telephone call to Attorney General Robert F. Kennedy. Then one of the riders led in singing freedom songs. Finally, as they sang "We are not afraid," National Guard troops arrived and broke up the mob with tear gas.

The frightening sounds faded away at last. But the town was so filled with hatred that Dr. King and the riders had to remain in the church basement most of the night. He told the riders that they must develop a quiet courage and be prepared to die for the cause if necessary.

Albany, Georgia, and Birmingham, Alabama

2

A FEW MONTHS LATER in Albany, Georgia, men, women, and children marched and joined sit-ins. More than 500 were arrested in three days. Dr. King and the Reverend Abernathy were among the first to be jailed. The Albany city officials refused to grant demands and called Dr. King a troublemaker.

This was the first defeat for Martin Luther King, Jr. But he learned a valuable lesson. He had tried to change the unfair laws in Albany with only a few hundred people. Now he realized that he needed thousands to fight for justice.

In April 1963, a thousand proud and angry marchers followed Dr. King and the Reverend Abernathy in Birmingham, Alabama, one of the worst Jim Crow cities in America. Nearly half of Birmingham's 600,000 citizens were Black, and they were demanding justice *now* because Birmingham was still disobeying the desegregation laws. They faced Eugene "Bull" Connor, the cruel white police chief. When the jails were filled, the police began using police dogs and fire hoses. The dogs growled and snapped at the marchers. And the powerful streams from the fire hoses beat the marchers against walls and to the ground. Thousands were thrown in jail, even some seven- and eight-year-old children. Sometimes Dr. King stopped to talk with the children, who asked him why they were treated this way. "Try not to hate—love will win," he would tell them.

While in the Birmingham jail, Dr. King had time to pray and to write. He sent a long letter to white ministers who had criticized him for moving too fast. He reminded them of the long suffering of Black people, even small children, and asked for their support.

Newspapers, radios, and television told the American people what was happening. They saw marchers clubbed and kicked, injured and bleeding. People all over the world became outraged. Now the Birmingham officials were forced to come to terms with Black leaders. On May 10, 1963, they agreed to end Jim Crow in Birmingham.

The March on Washington
(Backlash and Progress)

ℤ

SOON MARCHES and protests took place in 800 cities across the country. Then, on August 28, 1963, came the "March on Washington," planned by A. Philip Randolph and organized by Bayard Rustin. Led by Dr. King, the Reverend Abernathy, and other Black and white leaders, 250,000 people marched to Washington, D.C., to demand jobs and freedom. About one-fourth were white people who marched because they wanted a better America.

People arrived in Washington on foot, by bus, car, train, or plane. One young person skated from Chicago, Illinois. Some rolled along in wheelchairs, and others rode bicycles. Young white couples carried small children on their shoulders, while old people leaned on canes as they moved along. Rich and poor, Black and white marched quietly, under the hot sun, until they stood in front of the Lincoln Memorial. Many carried placards calling for full voting rights, jobs, and freedom. They wanted the same schools for Black and white children. The Supreme Court had outlawed separate schools in 1954, but some cities in the South were still ignoring the law.

The huge crowd listened to speeches and sang freedom songs. Roy Wilkins, from the NAACP, and Walter Reuther, from the AFL-CIO, spoke briefly. Mahalia Jackson moved the crowd with her gospel singing. And A. Philip Randolph told the people that this was just the first wave, that they must return home and continue to work for total freedom. Then the main speaker was presented—the Reverend Dr. Martin Luther King, Jr.

Dr. King stepped forward, the statue of Abraham Lincoln and the American flag in full view. His smile welcomed the marchers, but there was a trace of weariness on his face. It had been one hundred years since the freeing of the slaves, yet his people were still fighting for freedom. His voice rang out with great feeling:

"I have a dream today! I have a dream that someday little Black boys and little Black girls will join hands with little white boys and little white girls to work and play together. I have a dream today!"

Great cheers came from the crowd. He continued, "With faith we will be able to work together, to pray together, to struggle together, to go to jail together, knowing we will be free one day. Then we can join hands and sing the old Negro spiritual—

> Free at last, free at last,
> Great God Almighty,
> We are free at last."

The crowd clapped and cheered. Then they stood silent. They may never hear this kind of speech again. Thousands, including government officials and reporters, were in tears. Thousands more wept at home in front of their television sets. The great crowd of Black and white Americans joined hands and sang "We Shall Overcome." Then they turned and walked away with quiet dignity. The veteran leader A. Philip Randolph stood, with tears streaming down his face. Beside him stood Bayard Rustin.

Although millions of white Americans now believed in fair laws and were willing to obey them, there were many who wanted to prove that they could still keep the races separate. These included members of the Ku Klux Klan and Americans who lacked the courage to stand up for what was right. By the end of summer, young civil rights workers, both Black and white, had been killed; Medgar Evers, a Black leader, had been murdered; and a church had been bombed, killing four Black girls as they sat in Sunday school. Dr. King spoke of time running out. Freedom was not coming fast enough.

Coretta King had often marched by her husband's side, but now they had four children—Yolanda, Martin, Dexter, and Bernice—and she was needed at home. Dr. King had still less time for his family. When he wasn't traveling and marching, he was being followed or sitting in a bare jail cell. But on short, dangerous trips home, the Kings had good times together, reading, singing, and saying family prayers. Martin Luther King, Jr. laughed heartily as he romped and played with his children.

The King children worried when they heard of trouble or when they saw their father on television, being arrested and pushed about in a rough manner. But Mrs. King helped to keep them strong. She reminded them that his life was in constant danger and that he might leave home someday and never return.

In December, *Time* magazine named Martin Luther King, Jr. "Man of the Year" for 1963. This honor had been awarded for thirty-three years, but Dr. King was the first Black person to receive it. He could now become a very wealthy man if he chose to accept the offers that came to him. Instead, he stepped up protests and called for new and stronger national laws.

Dr. King began to fight against injustice and poverty for people of all races. He was constantly giving speeches against wars, especially the Vietnam war, which was costing so much money and taking so many lives for no just reason. Why couldn't this money be used to help poor people? He tried to convince his listeners that we could have a peaceful world if we were willing to work for it.

Before long, President Lyndon Johnson signed the Civil Rights bill that President John Kennedy had been working on. This 1964 law helped Blacks and other minorities to become first-class citizens. Among other things, it said:

> No one can be kept out of places such as hotels, lunch counters, gas stations, and theaters because of his race.

> No one can be kept out of public places such as parks, swimming pools, beaches, or libraries because of his race.

> Anyone who has passed the sixth grade in school must be allowed to vote without taking a test.

> The United States Attorney General can take school officials to court in places that still have segregated schools.

Dr. King was chosen to receive the Nobel Peace Prize in 1964. He had been given honors and prizes in the United States and in other countries. But this was the highest honor because it was presented each year, by the government of Norway, to the person who had done the most to bring about peace in the world. The King family flew to Oslo, Norway, where Dr. King received the prize at the University of Oslo on December 10, 1964. Only thirty-five years old and the youngest person to be given this honor, he stood on the platform with international leaders, kings, and queens to receive the gold medal, a diploma, and a prize of $54,600.

Dr. King gave the award money to the freedom movement because he said that all the people who worked for peace and brotherhood had earned the prize with him.

The Kings traveled to several European cities. They were greeted by royalty and cheered by crowds everywhere. Returning home, they were honored with a banquet in Atlanta by 1,500 Black and white citizens and entertained in other parts of the country. Mrs. King's heart was filled with gratitude. And the children were happy and proud of their father. But Dr. King wondered if this might be the time for him to step aside and let another leader take over. There had been so little time for family and friends, and there were increased threats on his life. His father, the Reverend Martin Luther King, Sr., had urged him to leave the front lines because of the danger. But Dr. King heard God say, "Go on, Martin." And he knew that he must continue to lead the way.

From Selma
to Montgomery

ϗ

IN SELMA, ALABAMA, the government ruling on voter registration was completely ignored. Half the citizens of Selma were Black, but only 300 Blacks were eligible to vote, compared to 10,000 white voters. Conditions were unbearable. A fifty-mile march from Selma, Alabama, to Montgomery, the state capital, was planned in protest. When the marchers attempted to cross the Edmund Petters Bridge, they were beaten and turned back by state troopers. Blacks, with white supporters, were clubbed and trampled by troops on horseback. Tear gas was used on others who tried to continue the march. It was a frightening scene, as television told the story.

Thousands marched to show support. White and Black people from all over the country went to Selma and offered to help. Soon, a court order gave permission for this historic march. Dr. and Mrs. King, with other leaders, led 3,000 on the last part of the five-day march. On March 25, 1965, they reached the white-domed capitol at Montgomery, where 25,000 people had gathered.

Before the march, President Johnson had asked Congress to pass a new voting rights bill, which became the Voting Rights Act of 1965. Signing it, the President said, "Today is a triumph for freedom." This bill gave more people voting rights and sent U.S. government workers out to enforce the law throughout the country.

Chicago,
North, East, and West

ʑ

IN JANUARY 1966, Dr. King turned his attention to Chicago and other cities where conditions had become deplorable. There were protests, marches, and boycotts. Riots broke out in cities across the country—Cleveland, Ohio; Harlem, New York; and Watts, California. Dr. King said he had never seen such hatred. Sometimes he visited A. Philip Randolph for advice. He was constantly called to help bring peace to trouble spots. Meanwhile, large numbers of his young followers felt that the nonviolent movement was not moving fast enough. They wanted justice now!

On a long, dusty road in Mississippi, a young man named Stokely Carmichael strode along at the head of a march. Suddenly he cried out, "Black Power!" The downtrodden Blacks repeated the call, "Black Power, Black Power!" These people didn't have power, but they were going to get it. They were going to take their rights.

Large numbers of young women and men, members of SNCC (Student Nonviolent Coordinating Committee), had criticized Dr. King's nonviolent plan as it was developing. They had worked with him since the beginning of the sit-ins. But even though they argued at times and disagreed with his direction, they continued to work and march with him throughout the long struggle.

Once Dr. King became angry at their impatience. "It takes time to change bad laws," he told the hurt and angry Blacks. "But you can still fight in a peaceful manner. Fight for 'green power'—money! You can't eat at a lunch counter or buy a car or a home without money. Nobody can be a first-class citizen unless he can live in dignity." The crowds listened. They hadn't gained anything by rioting or by burning their own houses and being clubbed by the police.

Poor People's March

BEFORE LONG, Martin Luther King, Jr. planned another march on Washington for all poor people. He and his staff called in leaders from different races to help plan this giant march. They all wanted a better life for the poor. But there was much argument about this march. Some thought nothing would be gained. But Dr. King was demanding new homes, apartments, parks, playgrounds, and modern shops. The ghettos must go this time! Everyone able to work must have a job, and the government must care for those unable to work. He called for action!

Before the march plans could be completed, another call came for help. Black garbage workers in Memphis, Tennessee, were striking for better working conditions and decent pay. Would Dr. King support them? Dr. King rushed to Memphis, where he led 6,000 people in a march for a better life. It was bitter cold, and tempers were on edge. Dr. King and other leaders walked with locked arms and sober faces. Still another threat was whispered against his life.

Suddenly, some young black militants, known as the Invaders, broke into the line and started to fight. They were encouraged by a police agent who wanted to break up the nonviolent march and defeat Dr. King's leadership. Many people were injured, and a seventeen-year-old Black boy was shot to death by the police. As National Guardsmen were called up to restore order, Dr. King was rushed to safety, and the march was halted. Not realizing what had happened, Dr. King wondered if his nonviolent method had failed. He and his men must return to Memphis and prove that people could protest in a peaceful manner.

On April 3, 1968, Dr. King returned to Memphis. That night he braved a storm to speak at a church. As the thunder rumbled, he told his people, "We've got to give ourselves to this struggle until the end. We've got some difficult days ahead. But it really doesn't matter with me now, because I've been to the mountaintop. And I've seen the Promised Land. I may not get there with you. But I want you to know tonight that we as a people will get to the Promised Land! So I'm happy tonight. I'm not worried about anything. I'm not fearing any man."

The Leader Is Slain

THE NEXT DAY Dr. King met with SCLC staff members at the Lorraine Motel, located a few blocks from downtown Memphis. Early that evening, he and the Reverend Abernathy talked as they dressed for dinner. Dr. King went out on the motel balcony.

A shadow moved in a room across the street, but no one noticed. Suddenly a shot cracked! Dr. King fell, a bullet hole in his neck. People began screaming and running about as policemen rushed up. They pointed across the way, to where they thought the shots had come.

The Reverend Abernathy knelt beside his friend. "Martin, Martin," he said. "This is Ralph. Martin, can you hear me?"

There was no answer. Martin Luther King, Jr., the peaceful leader, was dead.

The Reverend Andrew Young, a family friend, called Coretta King to tell her that her husband had been shot. News bulletins told the whole world of the tragedy. President Johnson spoke over nationwide television, asking that people be calm. "America is shocked and saddened," he said. Then he proclaimed a national day of mourning. And he ordered American flags lowered to half-staff on United States property everywhere in the world. Memorial services and marches were held in cities across the nation. Major league baseball delayed the opening games,

Rev. Martin Luther King, Jr., is shown riding a Montgomery, Alabama, bus up front on Friday, December 21, with the Rev. Glenn Smiley of Texas, a year after Dr. King lead the Montgomery bus boycott.

Dr. King meeting with President Kennedy and leaders of the March on Washington at the White House, August 8, 1963: *(left to right)* Whitney Young, Nation Urban League; Dr. King, Southern Leadership Conference; Rabbi Joachim Prinz, chairman of the American Jewish Congress; A. Philip Randolph, march director; President Kennedy; Walter Reuther, vice president of the AFL-CIO; and Roy Wilkins, NAACP

Leaders of the March on Washington lock arms and join hands as they move along Constitution Avenue, August 28, 1963. Dr. King is seventh from the right; A. Philip Randolph, march director, is at the far right.

Dr. King addressing a civil rights rally in Chicago that drew a crowd of over 70,000 to Soldier Field, June 21, 1964

Crown Prince Harald *(left)* and King Olav of Norway congratulate Dr. King and his wife after King was presented with the Nobel Peace Prize, Oslo, Norway, December, 1964.

Dr. King meeting in Washington, D.C., with Vice President Humphrey and Attorney General Katzenbach to discuss legislative steps needed to assure voting rights for Blacks

Dr. and Mrs. King push their way through a Chicago crowd after King had announced that Chicago would be the site of the first northern anti-slum drive, January, 1966.

Dr. King and Rev. Ralph Abernathy as they lead civil rights marchers out of camp on the second day of their Selma to Montgomery (Ala.) march, March 22, 1965

Mule-drawn caisson bearing the body of Dr. King moves up Auburn Avenue toward downtown Atlanta after funeral services for the slain civil rights leader, April 9, 1968

and men running for the presidency postponed their speeches. Messages of great sorrow came from all parts of the world.

Five days after the assassination, tens of thousands arrived in Atlanta for Dr. King's funeral. There were government officials, judges, and ministers of all races. Other prominent people attended, including then Vice-President Hubert H. Humphrey, Harry Belafonte, and Jacqueline Kennedy, widow of President John Kennedy, who had been assassinated in 1963.

During the service, the voice of Martin Luther King, Jr. rang out from a tape recording. It said, "If any of you are around when I have to meet my day, I don't want a long funeral. And if you get someone to give the eulogy, tell him not to talk too long. Tell him not to mention that I have a Nobel Peace Prize. That isn't important. Tell him not to mention that I have three or four hundred other awards. That's not important.

"I'd like someone to mention that day that Martin Luther King, Jr. tried to give his life serving others. I'd like for somebody to say that Martin Luther King, Jr. tried to love somebody—that I tried to love and serve humanity."

After the service, about 100,000 people marched five miles, under the scorching sun, behind an old green farm wagon drawn by two brown mules. The wagon, carrying Dr. King's casket, seemed to be a reminder of the poor and oppressed he had tried to help during his lifetime. Later that day, the casket was placed in a marble tomb on which were chiseled words of the Negro spiritual he loved and used in his Washington speech in 1963:

> "Free at last! Free at last!
> Thank God Almighty, I'm free at last."

Less than a month after the funeral, the Memphis garbage strike was settled with higher pay and union-regulated membership for the workers. And Congress

passed an improved housing law. The Poor People's
March on Washington, planned earlier by Dr. King,
brought together all of America's poor—the Puerto Ri-
cans, Asians, Indians, Mexican-Americans, poor Blacks,
and poor whites. Thousands came from all over the
country, on foot, in cars, and in buses. Led by the Reverend Jesse Jackson, of Operation Breadbasket, they
marched in the nation's capital to show the world that 40
million Americans were still struggling in poverty.

Setting up row upon row of tent homes or shanties to
create Resurrection City, these people waded through
mud day after day to make their voices heard. They had
been fighting to stay alive for so long and had been kept
apart, not trusting each other. Now they mingled and
shared their misery without thinking of race or color. In
Resurrection City, they saw for the first time how they
could unite in demanding a better life.

National leaders, embarrassed by the sad picture of
Resurrection City, tried to hurry the poor out of Washington. But a small victory was won when Congress
passed a one-million-dollar-a-year food program. A
number of bills were passed in the next few years, giving
those at the bottom new hope. The dreamer was dead,
but his dream lived on.

Where Is Justice?

𝕫

THE STATE OF Tennessee charged James Earl Ray with the killing of Dr. Martin Luther King, Jr. Ray, a white man, born in Alton, Illinois, had a history of crime, including robbery and burglary. The escape route of James Earl Ray in a white Mustang from Memphis, took him to Canada, England, Portugal and back to London. He had been given $20,000 to do a job. It wouldn't be difficult—he disliked Black people anyway. Ray had changed his name to Eric S. Galt and had a nose operation so he wouldn't be easily recognized. Still he was captured.

Back in the United States, Ray was tried and finally admitted killing Martin Luther King, Jr. A guilty verdict brought a ninety-nine-year prison term. Later, Ray fired his lawyers, claiming he didn't fire the fatal shot. People raised many questions. Was this horrible crime committed by one man, or were others involved? Eighty percent of those interviewed believed that Ray had not acted alone.

What was the motive for the killing? Many reasons were given—money interests, white racism, a plot by the FBI (Federal Bureau of Investigation) and the CIA (Central Intelligence Agency). It was learned that before Dr. King was awarded the Nobel Peace Prize in 1964, an FBI letter had warned him that he had only thirty-four days to live. And he had been followed all over Europe by agents of the CIA.

While James Earl Ray sat in his jail cell year after year, people continued to be concerned. Ray's lawyers wanted to appeal the case, hoping he could be set free. In 1975, a Senate committee asked former Attorney General Ramsey Clark to appoint a blue-ribbon commission to make a more thorough investigation of the King assassination, including any part the FBI and its chief, J. Edgar Hoover, might have played—members of the FBI and CIA had recently been accused of plotting the downfall of Dr. King. And, the Ku Klux Klan, working with various police departments in the South, had been accused by a former FBI agent of exchanging information and planning to defeat the civil rights movement. Testimony regarding these underground tactics was presented to a Congressional committee.

In May 1976, a United States Court of Appeals ruled that James Earl Ray could not change his confession that he killed Dr. King and that he could not have a retrial. Ray then planned to appeal his case to the United States Supreme Court in a final attempt to gain his freedom. And in September 1976, the U.S. House of Representatives voted to appoint a twelve-member committee to reopen the investigations in the assassinations of President John F. Kennedy and Dr. Martin Luther King, Jr.

People everywhere continue to remember this great man. Through all the misery and suffering in the nonviolent struggle for human and civil rights led by Dr. King, Black Americans held their heads high, realizing they were "as good and as smart as anybody." And millions of white Americans gained a new sense of brotherhood and became better human beings.

There are special ceremonies each year on January 15, Dr. King's birthday. And in many cities throughout the country, public and private schools are closed in his memory on that day. Congressman John Conyers, Jr. of

Michigan introduced a bill to make Dr. King's birthday a national holiday. Coretta King's program at the Martin Luther King, Jr. Center for Nonviolent Social Change in Atlanta, Georgia, is also gaining recognition. Mrs. King, with the help of millions of Americans, is working for full employment so that all people may live in dignity.

In July 1977, Martin Luther King, Jr. was posthumously awarded the presidential Medal of Freedom by President Jimmy Carter for his battle against prejudice. The President called Dr. King "the conscience of America."

There are still millions who hate people of other races. And greedy men who think to gain from bloody wars. But so long as there are followers in increasing numbers of this great, peaceful leader, we may believe that the dream of Martin Luther King, Jr. will someday come true.

BIBLIOGRAPHY

Bishop, Jim, *The Days of Martin Luther King, Jr.* New York: G. P. Putnam's Sons, 1971.

Franklin, John Hope, *Black Americans.* New York: Time-Life Books, 1973.

Katz, William L., *Eyewitness: The Negro in American History.* New York: Pitman Publishing Corporation, 1967.

King, Coretta Scott, *My Life with Martin Luther King, Jr.* New York: Holt, Rinehart & Winston, 1969.

King, Martin Luther, Jr., *Stride Toward Freedom.* New York: Harper & Brothers, 1958.

King, Martin Luther, Jr., *Why We Can't Wait.* New York: New American Library, 1964.

Peck, Ira, *The Life and Words of Martin Luther King, Jr.* New York: Scholastic Book Services, 1968.

Time-Life Books, eds., *I Have a Dream: The Story of Martin Luther King, Jr. in Text and Pictures.* New York: Time-Life Books, 1968.

Index